North Chicago Public Library

North Chicago, IL

GAYLORD

Keeping Students in School

Margaret Terry Orr

Foreword by Harold Howe II

Keeping Students in School

*A Guide to Effective
Dropout Prevention
Programs and Services*

Jossey-Bass Publishers

San Francisco • London • 1989

KEEPING STUDENTS IN SCHOOL
A Guide to Effective Dropout Prevention Programs and Services
by Margaret Terry Orr

Copyright © 1987 by: Jossey-Bass Inc., Publishers
350 Sansome Street
San Francisco, California 94104
&
Jossey-Bass Limited
28 Banner Street
London EC1Y 8QE

Library of Congress Cataloging-in-Publication Data

Orr, Margaret Terry, date.
   Keeping students in school.

   (The Jossey-Bass education series)
   Bibliography: p.
   Includes index.
   1. Dropouts—United States. 2. Students—Counseling
of—United States. 3. Dropouts—Employment—United
States. I. Title. II. Series.
LC131.077   1987   373.12'913   87-45502
ISBN 1-55542-070-2 (alk. paper)

Manufactured in the United States of America

The paper in this book meets the guidelines for
permanence and durability of the Committee on
Production Guidelines for Book Longevity of the
Council on Library Resources.

JACKET DESIGN BY WILLI BAUM

FIRST EDITION
   First printing: November 1987
   Second printing: July 1989

Code 8745

The Jossey-Bass
Education Series

Contents

Foreword

The United States has taken a route different from most European countries in guiding youth through the transition from schooling to work. The European model assumes that a high proportion of young people will leave school at age fifteen or sixteen. These young people are then offered an organized system of apprenticeships and other arrangements to serve their job preparation needs. A substantial proportion of young Europeans follow this route, entering training programs supported jointly by government and business.

The U.S. model assumes that all students will finish high school and then separate into two streams: those going to college and those going to work. We call those who leave school before graduation dropouts, thereby creating the impression that they have willfully rejected the opportunity to get a high school diploma and, consequently, to meet the requirement for most jobs. We recognized long ago that many young people did not succeed in high school and, therefore, needed an alternative means by which to achieve some recognition of adequate educational preparation to enter the job market. In response to this need, the General Educational Development test (GED) was created, and today, most states offer a diploma based on the results of this test. Military service or enrollment in a community college provide other entrances into the job market for U.S. youth who leave school. But, in the United States, there are no institutionalized, national or statewide programs designed to continue the education of young people who have not completed high school.

There are several good rationales behind the expectation that all U.S. youth should complete thirteen years of schooling. First, we consider thirteen years of mastering skills, gaining knowledge, and developing character and values to be basic building blocks in preparing citizens of our republic. Second, we have a strong interest in helping young citizens to reach their potential. We are willing to assume the expense of their education in order to allow our young people to discover their talents and interests. Third, we are committed to giving our young citizens an education that will provide each one with an equal opportunity for economic success. Tied to this third point is our need to compete in a world market that puts a premium on the job skills of our nation's work force.

In comparing the European and U.S. models, I take pride in the U.S. system. Our system offers all young people the possibility of seeking higher education, whereas the European system tends to place earlier limits on young people and to foster a tradition in which economic class controls educational opportunity. However, the U.S. model breaks down in the actual delivery of educational services. We have been only partly successful in providing schools that achieve our goals. And though our schools fail to adequately educate a large number of our young people, we have no alternate system for meeting their educational and employment needs. Indeed, even those who finish high school may flounder in the job market for several years after graduation, because, generally, we have no arrangements to help them find jobs.

Although the implication of the term *dropout* is that the student has left school willfully and without good reason, there is overwhelming evidence that many so-called dropouts leave because of the treatment they receive at school or the failure of school programs to meet their learning needs. In effect, these students are forced out. Other evidence suggests that many dropouts face personal and economic conditions that seriously limit the possibility of their continuation or success in school.

Educators in the United States have become increasingly active in working with dropouts: They are trying to improve their schools' programs in order to increase student success and, thereby, reduce the number of dropouts; and they are seeking new ways to reconnect students who have already dropped out with the job and higher education opportunities promised by success in high school. Through these two endeavors, our educators are not only attempting to live up to the U.S. assumption that all young people should finish high school, they are also trying to establish a U.S. equivalent to the European assumption that students who leave school will need continuing educational services if they are ever to succeed in the job market.

Keeping Students in School will serve as an invaluable tool for educators, school board members, or state officials who are in the process of thinking through these issues. The book presents a useful picture of what is going on in the United States today in the dual realms of dropout prevention and dropout rescue. It discusses initiatives that have originated at the state, school district, and individual school levels. And it provides specific information about fourteen programs, including some that involve important cooperation between public schools and private business, and others that have been initiated by agencies in the employment and training field.

The author, Margaret Terry Orr, and her associates have visited each of the fourteen programs described in the book to get firsthand information. These various programs reflect what is needed for service efforts to be most successful and illustrate a great variety of strategies that can be employed to deal with dropout issues. The programs are tailored to the needs of the youth they serve: They emphasize learning and job skills, and they offer the potential dropout and the student who has already dropped out critically needed encouragement and practical services, such as day-care programs for teenage mothers.

While in many ways the youth dropout problem can be addressed through changes in our educational system, the responsibility for helping dropouts toward some constructive path lies with many groups. Significant contributions in support and design of programs can be made by federal, state, and local governments. Individual schools and community agencies can offer a range of assistance for at-risk and out-of-school youth. Parents and even local businesses can be usefully enlisted in this cause. *Keeping Students in School* can instruct these groups about where and how to begin.

Cambridge, Massachusetts   Harold Howe II
September 1987   *Senior Lecturer,*
                                                    Graduate School of Education,
                                                    Harvard University

Preface

Although our nation's school dropout rate has remained unchanged over the past twenty years, increasing demands from new high-tech industries for a better prepared and better educated work force have changed the way we view this problem. As a result, policy makers, planners, and program operators from the education and employment and training arenas are searching for ways to prevent students from dropping out and to prepare actual dropouts educationally and vocationally.

Identifying what can be done programmatically is the first step toward a solution. *Keeping Students in School* demonstrates how programs can be designed, implemented, and operated through collaborative initiatives and funding. By presenting a planning framework and in-depth program illustrations, this book shows what schools, public agencies, and communities can do to tackle their dropout problem.

I have authored this book under the auspices of the Structured Employment/Economic Development Corporation (SEEDCO), a New York-based nonprofit organization that designs, manages, and evaluates economic development and employment projects. SEEDCO has extensively evaluated the impact of federal job training programs in serving disadvantaged

xv

groups, particularly youth dropouts. At SEEDCO, extensive research on the dropout phenomenon has shown that leaving
school early is related to many problems, only some of which
can be addressed by schools. Schools can provide targeted programs and revamp the delivery of educational services, but, as
the book shows, the resources of other public and private agencies are also needed to support students at risk of dropping out
and to help those who have left school to obtain an education
and prepare for work. *Keeping Students in School* illustrates the
various roles social agencies, local businesses, and government
entities must play in tackling this large educational problem.

The book is designed around a planning framework that
is concerned with two categories of youth: those who are at risk
of dropping out and those who have already left school. The
different personal situations of young people also have a bearing
on what kind of program support will be appropriate to help
each one complete their high school education. For example,
young people who lack direction and self-esteem can benefit
from peer group counseling; migrant youth who must work can
continue school through an evening instructional program.

This book is intended to serve several audiences. Public
school system principals, superintendents, and other school program administrators, as well as funders and administrators of
public and private employment and training programs, will find
this book an important resource when addressing their dropout
problems. It is also a useful planning guide for policy makers—
legislators and their staff members, federal and state education
and labor agency officials, policy board members from state and
local boards of education, and members of private industry and
community planning councils. Finally, the book can serve as a
forum for discussion and organization for related interest
groups, including community agencies, parent groups, advocacy
organizations, and professional and other member associations.

Overview of the Contents

Because the youth dropout problem cannot be resolved
in a piecemeal fashion, *Keeping Students in School* is not limited to describing discrete programs. The book also includes

examples of systemic change in the operations, instruction methods, curriculum, and program offerings of school systems. The objective of this kind of change is to expand learning opportunities for all youth and to benefit those at risk of dropping out, in particular. The book also contains a discussion of critical program features and approaches.

Chapter One sets the stage for thinking about services for potential and actual dropouts by reviewing available research and demographic information. It offers extensive evidence on the scope and nature of the dropout problem and the current public policy concerns that make the need for its resolution so immediate.

In Chapter Two, I review what is known about services for the potential and actual dropout populations, based on experience in compensatory education, alternative programs, and employment and training services. Findings from these programs are evaluated together with suggestions about necessary and ideal program features. And these suggestions are combined with an assessment of the target groups for dropout prevention and service efforts.

Chapters Three through Eight present in-depth descriptions of fourteen variously structured programs for potential dropouts and out-of-school youth. Each description covers the program's design, its target population and curriculum, its administration and funding, and the available evidence concerning its effectiveness. Together these six chapters form the extensive outline of a program planning framework. The programs are presented in sequence from those that offer the least intervention to those that offer the most—from supplemental to comprehensive. And they serve a continuum of young people—from those who need encouragement to stay in school or need to develop self-esteem to those who have already left school and must complete their education through alternate routes.

In Chapter Three, I describe three programs that use supplemental service approaches—a program of peer-group counseling run by a community agency, a mentoring program sponsored by a professional association, and a summer youth employment program. The three programs discussed in Chapter Four illustrate possible solutions to the barriers to continuing education for youth by providing on-site day-care services or comprehensive health-care services, or by scheduling evening classes for employed migrant youth.

Chapter Five contains descriptions of three comprehensive school-affiliated programs for potential dropouts and, in Chapter Six, I cover two programs for out-of-school youth. The three school-based programs described in Chapter Five include a department store–based alternative program; a rural, alternative school with an occupationally focused program; and a school within a school for entering ninth graders, cosponsored by a business group. In Chapter Six, the two programs for out-of-school youth include a network of educational clinics sponsored by a state government and a network of alternative schools and youth centers. Both of these programs help school dropouts to prepare for the GED and future employment.

Chapter Seven explains the systemwide approach to dropout prevention using the experiences of two urban systems. One program, initiated by the New York City school system, set minimum dropout rate levels for all high schools and provided an approach for secondary schools to deal with poor student attendance. Another comprehensive program in Los Angeles has supported targeted elementary and secondary schools in designing their own solutions to the dropout problem and school administrators in exploring ways to expand educational opportunities for all students. In Chapter Eight, the approach taken in a third city illustrates a similar, but more comprehensive, community effort. The Boston school system has created a formal role for local businesses, universities, and trade unions that can lend resources and expand post–high school opportunities for all students. At the same time, the school system has created a dropout prevention task force, which reviews the system's delivery of educational services and alternative training solutions.

Chapter Nine is a synthesis of the various lessons learned from the fourteen programs and includes suggestions concerning program design, common service strategies, and methods for funding and management. I also review the evidence of program effectiveness and stress the importance of evaluation for discovering what works under which circumstances. The chapter concludes with a review of the book's findings and their implications for the broader educational system and the employment and training field.

Acknowledgments

The facts and programs presented in *Keeping Students in School* are a compilation of information from a wide range of sources. Over fifty educators, planners, and researchers participated in the conceptualization of this book by recommending programs for study. Staff members from the fourteen programs described in the book generously provided their time to demonstrate their programs, share their knowledge, answer endless questions, and review draft summaries. James Meier, Hannah Rosen, Katherine Solow, and John Whalen assisted in reviewing and documenting each program.

SEEDCO's former president, William Grinker, provided invaluable supervision and guidance throughout the development and compilation of the manuscript. And through his continuation of that support, James Pickman, SEEDCO's current president, ensured that the book would be completed. Ron Monroe and Joan Woodbridge undertook the numerous details involved in producing successive drafts. And Mary Lutton O'Connor's copyediting guaranteed consistency in the style and structure of the final manuscript.

An advisory group—with representatives from national organizations, agencies, and universities concerned about the dropout problem—assisted in researching the fourteen programs and producing the manuscript. I thank the following people for their advice and recommendations: Terry Clark, New York University; Evelyn Ganzglass, National Governors' Association; Clifford Johnson, Children's Defense Fund; Rodney Riffel, National Conference of State Legislatures; Andrew Sum, Northeastern University; and Gary Wehlage, University of Wisconsin. A substantive review of the early drafts of some chapters was completed by Gordon Berlin, Sharon Franz, Edward Meade, Anthony Proscio, Gary Walker, and Robin Willner.

Most important, the research and production of the report that lead to *Keeping Students in School* was supported by a generous grant from the Carnegie Corporation of New York. (The content of this book does not necessarily reflect the views of the Carnegie Corporation.) Program officers Diane August and Vivien Stewart were very helpful throughout the preparation of that report.

New York, New York   Margaret Terry Orr
September 1987

The Author

Margaret Terry Orr is a senior associate with Structured Employment/Economic Development Corporation (SEEDCO). She received her B.A. degree in sociology from Denison University and her M.A. degree in educational administration and Ph.D. degree in educational policy planning and research from Columbia University. Orr's main research interests have been the policies and programs that affect adolescents, including educational programs, access and availability of family planning, and federal and other publicly funded job training services. Currently, she is investigating the state and local coordination of the federal Job Training Partnership Act and other public education services designed to address the training needs of youth dropouts. Orr is also adjunct assistant professor in the Department of Educational Administration at Teachers College, Columbia University.

Keeping Students
in School

1

Understanding the Dropout Problem: What Are the Causes and Who Are the Casualties?

It is estimated that as many as 25 percent of the students who enter high school each year will not graduate. Instead, these young people, who are primarily urban and economically disadvantaged, become school dropouts. Their economic and social opportunities have become increasingly bleak over the past twenty years as business and industry have come to require a more literate and highly trained work force. To increase the proportion of young people who graduate from high school, educators and other policy and program officials have started to examine why youth drop out. By learning why students leave, it has been reasoned, we can more ably design programs that will help them to stay.

Definition of a Dropout

A dropout is a student who withdraws from school without a high school diploma and without enrolling elsewhere. Despite the intensity of public attention to the nation's dropout rate, estimates of the number of youth who drop out are conflicting and inconclusive.

Schools and communities lack a uniform definition of

what a youth dropout is and when someone is officially recognized as a dropout. One reason is that being a dropout is not a clear status. Students may be absent for extended periods or may withdraw or transfer without notifying the school. School systems use different accounting methods to estimate the number of dropouts, reflecting differences in policies on when students can officially withdraw from school before graduation. They also vary widely in acknowledging as dropouts the many students who attend school rarely or who leave without official notification and without enrolling elsewhere. In addition, many dropouts may later reenroll in high school, attend other education and training programs, join the military, or obtain a General Equivalency Diploma (GED), thereby changing their dropout status. It is important, however, to determine how many students quit school before graduating, because that number represents the total need for dropout services.

Education professionals, policy makers, and government officials are now working on a standard definition of a school dropout that will allow comparisons among school districts and states. In the absence of this single clear definition, the best estimates of the number dropping out must come from various national sample and census population surveys. These estimates range from 14 to 25 percent. They vary widely because the surveys on which they are based either are different point-in-time calculations of youth and adults who state that they are dropouts or are comparisons of enrollment and graduation figures. While these estimates provide insight into the scope of the dropout problem—especially the characteristics of those who leave and the regions in which they live—they fall short of describing comprehensively who drops out. These problems should be considered when using the information.

Scope of the Problem

The most recent information on the extent of the dropout problem comes from the 1985 Current Population Survey (CPS). These data show that 4.3 million sixteen- to twenty-four-year-olds were dropouts in October 1985 (U.S. General Accounting Office, 1986). This number represents 13 percent of all youth in that age-group and includes 14 percent of all eighteen- and nineteen-year-olds. These percentages differ little from CPS estimates made since 1975. This census underestimates the dropout problem, however, since it identifies only those who have already dropped out, not those who might drop out in the future, and it excludes youth who dropped out of school but have since obtained a GED or otherwise completed their high school education.

The CPS estimates are similar to the findings of the High School and Beyond Survey, a longitudinal survey begun in 1980 of a randomly selected sample of 30,000 sophomores from over one thousand public and private high schools (Peng, 1983). The High School and Beyond Survey showed that 14 percent of 1980 sophomores dropped out before their expected graduation in 1982. This includes 12 percent of white, 17 percent of black, and 19 percent of Hispanic sophomores. The survey understates the number of school dropouts, however, because it does not include those who left school before becoming sophomores. Unlike the CPS, it includes all sophomores who ever dropped out, regardless of whether they eventually returned to school or attained a GED.

A third estimate comes from the National Longitudinal Survey, a longitudinal study of over 12,000 randomly selected young men and women fourteen to twenty-one years old begun in 1979 (Baker and others, 1984). This study shows slightly higher dropout estimates, especially for Hispanics. It found that 15 percent of the youth who were twenty-one between 1979 and 1982 had not yet completed high school, including 12 percent of white, 23 percent of black, and 36 percent of Hispanic youth. Like the CPS, the National Longitudinal Survey underestimates the school dropout rate because it counts only those who are out of school and who do not have a GED or a high school diploma. Unlike the High School and Beyond Survey, however, it is not limited to those who had reached their sophomore year. It is unclear why the estimates of Hispanic dropouts are so much higher in this survey. One explanation may be that a substantial portion of the Hispanic dropouts left before their sophomore year and thus were not included in the High School and Beyond Survey estimates.

In contrast to the findings from these sample surveys, national public school enrollment data suggest that 25 percent of students entering ninth grade never graduate, including as many as 50 percent of the students in inner-city high schools (U.S. General Accounting Office, 1986). These percentages are calculated by comparing the total number of graduating students in a given year with the number enrolled in ninth grade four years earlier; the difference is assumed to be the number of dropouts. This method overestimates the number who drop out because it does not take into account the number of students who graduate at a faster or slower pace. It also counts as dropouts those who left high school without graduating but obtained a GED or went into the military or a job training program.

Using these approximations, it can be estimated that as few as 470,000 or as many as 830,000 of the 3.3 million students who entered ninth grade in the fall of 1983 will drop out before their scheduled graduation in the spring of 1987 (Office of Educational Research and Improvement, 1986). More startling is the estimate that from 2.3 to 4.2 million of all youth between eighteen and twenty-one in 1983 had been or still were high school dropouts. Even the lowest estimate of the dropout rate represents a substantial educational and societal problem.

Characteristics of Dropouts

Some students are more likely than others to become dropouts. The High School and Beyond Survey has extensively tracked both graduates and dropouts of the 1980 class of sophomores. While that survey underestimates the total number of dropouts, various analyses of its data set provide extensive information about those who have dropped out. According to those figures, youth dropouts are concentrated in urban areas: urban youth are 50 percent more likely to drop out than youth living in rural areas. Regional differences vary by race: whites in the South and West are more likely to drop out than those in the Northeast and North Central states, while the reverse is true for blacks. Few regional differences exist for Hispanic youth (Peng, 1985).

Those who are the least prepared economically and educationally are the most likely to drop out. Twenty-two percent of students from low-income families, but only 7 percent of those from high-income families, drop out of school. Similarly, students who score low on achievement tests are six times as likely to drop out as those whose scores are high. In addition, 27 percent of the sophomores who have repeated at least one grade, in contrast to 12 percent of those who have not, later drop out. Those students who are overage when beginning ninth grade are far more likely than their classmates fourteen and younger to leave school without graduating. Finally, the relationship between an adolescent's educational attainment and that of his or her parents cannot be ignored: those students whose fathers or mothers never completed high school are about twice as likely as other students to drop out (Barro, 1984).

Dropouts are more likely than their graduating peers to have had school attendance and discipline problems while enrolled (Barro, 1984). Eighty-two percent of sophomores who later drop out, in contrast to 93 percent of those who do not, attend classes regularly. Those who have been suspended, have been put on probation, or have had serious trouble with the law are three times as likely to drop out as are those who have not.

Involvement in extracurricular activities can encourage students to remain in school, but only up to a point. Students who participate in extracurricular activities, particularly athletics, are less likely than others to drop out (Weber, 1986). But students who work fifteen or more hours per week while attending school are at least 50 percent more likely to drop out than those who work less or not at all (Barro, 1984).

In-depth statistical investigation has shown that educational and economic background together are the strongest determinants of whether a student will drop out of school. When these factors are taken into consideration, racial and ethnic differences are no longer significant (U.S. General Accounting Office, 1986).

Causes of Dropping Out

While poor academic performance and a low-income background make a student more likely to leave school, they are not the causes of dropping out. After all, 73 percent of students who have repeated a grade and 78 percent of those from low-income families successfully complete high school (Barro, 1984). Poor academic performance and poverty encompass many personal and social pressures that have long been known to be impediments to educational achievement. These pressures and other factors may be the actual causes of dropping out. Only limited investigations of the causes have been made, however, and those rely upon students' own explanations.

Findings from the High School and Beyond Survey illustrate the reasons adolescents commonly give for dropping out (Peng, 1983). Most cited school-related problems, including having poor grades, having discipline problems, not getting along with teachers, and generally not liking school. They also identified family-related problems, such as getting married, being pregnant, and needing to work. Less frequently, they mentioned personal problems, such as being sick or responding to peer pressure. Adolescent men were much more likely to cite school-related problems (36 percent had poor grades, 21 percent could not get along with teachers, and 13 percent were expelled or suspended) or deciding to work (27 percent). Adolescent women were more likely to cite marital or parenthood reasons (31 and 23 percent, respectively) for dropping out, but they also had school-related problems (31 percent stated that school was "not for them" and 30 percent had poor grades).

It is evident that the explanations given by dropouts are insufficient, since other students with the same kinds of problems remain. It may be that a combination of problems, the severity of a single problem, or the unavailability of alternatives is the deciding factor in leaving school.

The students' explanations show that both school and external factors have a critical effect on whether students remain in and complete high school, but how much of a part each factor plays is unclear. Other research has tried to document their effects. For example, research on academic achievement has found that during the school year, economically advantaged and disadvantaged youth achieve at similar rates. But economically disadvantaged youth, unlike their more advantaged peers, lose some of their academic gains over the summer; this indicates the significant role of the family and community in learning and achievement (Berlin and Sum, 1986).

Other researchers have tried to investigate how much schools alienate students, discouraging them from staying in school (Bullis, 1986; Hammond and Howard, 1986; Mann, 1986; Wehlage, 1986). Their research suggests that schools send signals to poorly achieving students and those who are discipline problems, in a sense urging them to leave. This lack of encouragement may compound a student's personal and family problems, further reducing any desire or ability to remain in school.

Consequences of Dropping Out

Once out of school, youth dropouts have two options. They can complete their education by returning to school or by obtaining their GED, or they can try to support themselves through employment or other means.

Many young dropouts eventually pursue the first option. The High School and Beyond Survey results indicate that at least half of youth dropouts try to complete their education. Of the 1980 sophomores who dropped out, 10 percent had returned to school or obtained their GED by the spring of 1982, when their class was to graduate. By 1984, up to half the dropouts had reentered school or were in GED classes, and 38 percent had finally graduated. The survey results showed that whites were more likely than blacks and Hispanics to return and finish —41 percent in contrast to 33 and 30 percent, respectively (Kolstad and Owings, 1986).

Overall, those whose academic and personal backgrounds made them least likely to be dropouts were most likely to return or get their GED (Kolstad and Owings, 1986). That is, dropouts who had higher achievement test scores, post–high school plans, and families with higher incomes were more likely than other dropouts to return and to finish high school. Certainly, prior educational gains make it easier for returning dropouts to obtain a GED or complete their education, and concrete plans are a strong motivation for finishing school. Those who did return were more likely as eighteen- or nineteen-year-olds to be enrolled in the military or a postsecondary program or to be employed than were dropouts who did not return.

For most youth dropouts, the lack of a diploma limits employment options and thus future economic and social conditions. Overall, dropouts are more likely than their peers who have graduated not to be in the labor force; if employed, they are more likely to have semiskilled manual jobs and to earn less. The disparity is even greater among blacks than among whites.

According to the CPS of October 1985, 68 percent of high school dropouts and 87 percent of graduates between the ages of sixteen and twenty-four were in the labor market (U.S. General Accounting Office, 1986). Of these, one in four of the dropouts, but just one in ten of the high school graduates, was unemployed. The disparity in the employment opportunities for graduates and dropouts is illustrated best by the percentage employed in technical, administrative support, and sales occupations: just 8 percent of the male dropouts, but 20 percent of the male graduates, were so employed.

These limited employment options are evident in differences in salary and cumulative lifetime earnings. The CPS data show that the median income of dropouts twenty-five and older in 1984 was 30 percent lower than the income of high school graduates. The expected lifetime earnings of high school dropouts were about one-third lower than those of high school graduates and half those of college graduates (Berlin, 1984). Current male dropouts will lose an average of $266,000 and female dropouts $199,000 in earnings over their lifetimes (Catterall, 1985).

As interviews performed in the High School and Beyond Survey show, the limits of their employment opportunities were already obvious to the dropouts. As of the spring of 1982, 27 percent of the males and 21 percent of the females were unemployed, dissatisfied with their work, or looking for work. Only 66 percent of the males and 31 percent of the females were in full- or part-time jobs. About 53 percent regretted their decision to leave school prematurely (Owings and Kolstad, 1985).

Dropping out is costly not only to the individual but to

society. For the dropouts of the high school class of 1981, potential lifetime earnings lost total $228 billion; the lost tax revenues from these earnings are approximately $68.4 billion (Catterall, 1985). Because they suffer from reduced employment opportunities, dropouts require more welfare, health care, and unemployment subsidies. They are more likely to be involved in criminal activities, thus incurring costs for judicial and penal services. Public expenditures for welfare, health care, and police that can be attributed to school dropouts are estimated to be from $10 to $29 billion annually (Catterall, 1985).

Helping a greater proportion of potential dropouts to complete their education can reduce such costs substantially. Projecting from a national sample of youth, researchers have estimated that if all nineteen- to twenty-three-year-olds were to obtain high school diplomas, the probability of their having out-of-wedlock births would decrease by over 50 percent and that of being arrested by over 90 percent. The likelihood of their being welfare-dependent would decrease by almost one-tenth (Berlin and Sum, 1986). These savings far outweigh the costs of helping these students to complete school.

Policy Issues and Responses

Beyond the individual and societal costs of our youth dropout problem, several educational and economic concerns have stirred policy responses. These concerns center on the educational achievements of our youth, the projected decline in the size and capability of our work force, and the reduced employment opportunities for young adults who lack a high school diploma.

Our country has come to recognize the relationship between educational preparation and economic productivity (Berlin and Sum, 1986). Our students, however, are undereducated and under-performing in mathematics and the sciences. In a mathematical proficiency test, U.S. high school seniors ranked lowest among students from all industrialized countries; Japanese students scored the highest. To ensure a competitive work force, therefore, our country must "stiffen the rigors, quality

and quantity of high school education for all American youth"
(Berlin and Sum, 1986, p. 18).

Numerous calls for reform—best exemplified by the 1983
National Commission on Excellence in Education report, *A
Nation at Risk*—have recommended that educational standards
and high school graduation requirements be upgraded. These
various reports have highlighted the declining quality of education nationwide and its costs to our country's industries and
world leadership. By 1985, all states had at least considered
more rigorous grade promotion and graduation requirements for
students and a system to hold districts accountable for poor student performance (National Coalition of Advocates for Students,
1985). Local school districts also responded with stricter minimum performance standards for promotion and graduation.

Critics of these reforms cite how little they have addressed
the educational needs of disadvantaged students (Cusick, 1984;
Goodwin and Muraskin, 1985; McDill, Natriello, and Pallas,
1985; National Coalition of Advocates for Students, 1985).
Their primary complaint is that such reforms may discourage
more students and cause them to drop out of school. A fall
1985 survey of fifty-four state educational commissions in
thirty-two states found that less than one-fourth mentioned assisting disadvantaged youth; just four commissions made recommendations about economically disadvantaged youth and six
commissions addressed underachieving youth (MDC, Inc., 1985).

In a different approach, the National Coalition of Advocates for Students held hearings in ten cities on the problems of
adequately educating all children. In its 1985 report, the coalition recommends that educational improvement not be made
by raising standards or by putting at-risk students, including
potential dropouts, into special programs. It recommends instead the removal of school-imposed barriers to learning (such
as inflexible school structures and narrow curricula and teaching
practices) and the recognition that many students need extra
help to realize their academic potential.

While educators have been reviewing educational standards, economists and demographers have become increasingly
concerned about the impact on the labor market of changes in

the demographic composition of our labor force and school population and in how well subgroups are educated. The decline in our youth population, coupled with the growing proportion of that population that belongs to minority and disadvantaged groups and is thus more likely to be poorly educated, projects a dim picture of the future productivity of the labor market (Levin, 1985).

From 1970 to 1980, the U.S. school enrollment dropped from 46 to 41 million, while the percentage of students who belong to minority groups increased from 21 to 27 percent. This shift in the racial and ethnic composition of our school population is critical, because minority students are more likely than others to be economically disadvantaged. Moreover, the proportion of minority children who live in poor families has been increasing, from 16 percent in 1979 to 22 percent in 1983. Thus, over the next few decades, greater percentages of school-age children will be economically disadvantaged. This characteristic is highly correlated with experiencing educational problems; more supplemental school programs will therefore be needed to assist these students in keeping up academically (Levin, 1985).

Meanwhile, it is obvious that business and industry need the labor force to be more prepared educationally, not less. Over the past ten to twenty years, real mean earnings have declined. These declines have disproportionately affected those with the least education, who are employed less often and usually receive lower hourly wages. The difference in income between male high school dropouts and graduates aged eighteen to twenty-four nearly doubled between the early 1960s and the early 1980s, growing from 31 to 59 percent (Berlin and Sum, 1986). Clearly, employers are placing a greater importance on educational performance, particularly attainment of a high school diploma.

Economists and other forecasters now argue that as the disadvantaged become a majority of the public school population, their educational problems and the consequences of them become a concern of the more advantaged as well. One observer has said that if these problems are ignored, society as a whole will become less economically competitive, as industries spend more on training and lose more in productivity, and will spend more on public services for poverty, crime prevention, and re-habilitation, as a greater segment of the population becomes un-employable (Levin, 1985).

In anticipation of these problems, states and local com-munities have begun to explore ways of preventing students from dropping out. While the nature and scope of new policies and programs have not yet been summarized and quantified, the most common approach has been to add new program funding generally or to direct funds specifically to dropout-prone stu-dents. While such funding is often limited in scope—one typical urban district allocated substantial new program funds that averaged only fifty dollars per dropout (Catterall, 1985)—it pro-vides a useful starting point for planning and designing dropout prevention measures.

Conclusions

It is surprising that with all the available technology, we are unable to estimate accurately how many students leave school early. But extensive longitudinal studies show which types of youth are most at risk, so planning and targeting ser-vices are feasible.

The causes of dropping out are numerous and stem from many of the economic and social circumstances that are closely related to other youth problems, including adolescent parent-hood, unemployment, drug abuse, and crime. Unless the school environment and instructional programs are responsive to these negative circumstances, they can actually reduce a student's chances of remaining in school.

Clearly both school and external factors can cause stu-dents to drop out, although the extent to which each contrib-utes is little understood. Yet even without more in-depth re-search on the causes of dropping out, program planning need not be postponed but can begin to help more students remain in school and serve those who have already left.

2

How Schools and Communities Can Address the Dropout Problem

From a review of the scope and nature of the youth dropout problem, several program planning features are obvious. This problem stems from many causes; it exists in many forms and many degrees of severity; several program solutions are therefore needed. And because the sources of the problem are the responsibility of many service systems, the solutions ought to come from many areas.

The climate for developing solutions to the dropout problem is good. Heightened public attention to what is now recognized as a crisis in education has triggered widespread and varied responses. School systems, social agencies, and communities are assessing the need and the resources available for dropout prevention and service programs. States and local areas are allotting new funds for attendance improvement and dropout prevention. But despite the severity of the school dropout problem and the widespread concern over resolving it, scant information exists on solutions.

Dropout prevention and service programs are not new. Youth dropouts have typically been one of many target groups for public school alternative programs and employment and training programs. Unfortunately, these programs have never

been widely available. But information about them, combined
with a better understanding of the characteristics and problems
of youth dropouts, will provide a basis for designing and implementing program solutions.

Background

Until recently, only three general approaches to serving
youth dropouts and potential dropouts existed: compensatory
education, alternative education, and employment and training
programs. Despite the wide range of programs in each category,
available research offers only limited insight into which program
designs might work. It is nonetheless useful to review what is
known about these three approaches to determine the most effective ways to build on them.

Compensatory Education. Substantial federal, state, and
local funding has been directed to providing reading and math
assistance to economically disadvantaged youth experiencing
academic problems. The largest portion by far has come from a
federal program, Chapter 1 of the Education Consolidation and
Improvement Act (before 1982, Title I of the Elementary and
Secondary Education Act). This funding reaches 68 percent of
all public elementary schools, including 90 percent of schools in
which more than half of the students are disadvantaged (National Coalition of Advocates for Students, 1985). While Chapter 1 provides only funding, leaving the individual schools to devise their own services, limited evaluations have demonstrated
the program's effectiveness in improving reading and math
achievement for participants. The program has so far had limited success in reducing the achievement test score gap between
white and nonwhite students over time, but much more funding
and many more programs are needed.

Despite substantial funding, the available compensatory
education programs do not meet the need. The cost of early
intervention has been calculated to be one-sixth the cost of having a child repeat a grade. Yet of the 8–10 million students (20–
25 percent of all public school children) who were eligible for

Title I in 1980-81, only half were served, including only a few high school students (National Coalition of Advocates for Students, 1985). In the 1970s, Title I funding typically made up only about 3 percent of all elementary and secondary education expenditures in the United States (Levin, 1985). Funding was reduced when Title I was replaced with Chapter 1. As the disadvantaged student population increases and funding decreases, these nominal resources will be spread even more thinly and any possible impact will be weakened further.

Alternative Education. Public school systems commonly offer alternative programs for special-needs students, who range from the gifted and talented to the emotionally or learning disabled. Students at risk of dropping out have often been targeted for alternative programs. These programs have been funded by a range of federal, state, and local sources. Title VIII of the Elementary and Secondary Education Act provided from $5 to $10 million per year between 1968 and 1976 for dropout prevention programs in public schools with high dropout rates and high concentrations of students from low-income families. A federal evaluation found that most projects were effective in reducing the dropout rate. The federal program funding was later absorbed into a new consolidated program. Although districts could continue to use the funds for dropout prevention programs, there is no information on whether they did (Lyke, 1985).

While no large-scale study of alternative school programs for youth dropouts exists, there is some evidence of their effectiveness. Educational researchers have analyzed longitudinal survey data on a randomly selected national sample of high school students and dropouts, focusing on a subset living in California and enrolled in alternative education programs (Catterall and Stern, 1986). The researchers assumed that the subset was representative of the state, but they caution that their findings may be susceptible to sampling error. Because California state law establishes minimum criteria and overriding goals for alternative programs, the researchers thought the programs would be similar enough to allow comparison of enrollments in alternative programs and the likelihood of dropping out. Their results showed that of sophomores who thought they might not finish high school, those who participated in alternative programs were half as likely to drop out eventually as those who did not. Even more impressive were the post–high school benefits: graduates who had been in alternative programs had a 20 percent lower unemployment rate than dropouts who had not participated in these programs.

Other reviews of dropout prevention programs have been limited to discussions of individual programs or identification of promising program practices (Appalachian Regional Commission, 1985; Institute for Educational Leadership, 1986; National Center for Research in Vocational Education, 1986; National Coalition of Advocates for Students, 1985; Treadway, 1985; and Wehlage, 1986). Their recommendations most often include the following: that the program be small; that it be in a nontraditional setting; that it foster a close working relationship between staff and students, emphasizing support and encouragement; that it employ a comprehensive and multifaceted service approach; that it emphasize improvement of basic skills and self-esteem; and that work experience or other types of experiential learning be included. As yet, however, no evaluation has tested the effectiveness of these program characteristics in keeping potential dropouts in school.

Employment and Training Programs. With a mixture of federal and other public and private funding, economically disadvantaged youth and adults and those who have difficulty finding employment (which includes youth dropouts) are offered training, employment preparation, and job placement through highly decentralized and diverse public employment and training programs. The principal federal support for these efforts is the Job Training Partnership Act (JTPA), which replaced the Comprehensive Employment and Training Act (CETA) in 1981.

During the middle and late 1970s, the Department of Labor, through CETA, funded several demonstration youth programs to determine which employment and training strategies were effective. Large-scale evaluations of these programs provide the most conclusive evidence of what works in serving potential and actual youth dropouts. Between 1979 and 1981, over 6,000 in-school and out-of-school youth participated in one of six programs: Youth Employment and Training Programs; Youth Community Conservation and Improvement Projects; Youth Incentive Entitlement Pilot Projects; Young Adults Conservation Corps; Job Corps; and Summer Youth Employment Programs (Betsey, Hollister, and Papageorgiou, 1985). The programs were designed to encourage young people to return to and complete high school by offering them temporary jobs; the work experience prepared them for future employment.

While each program model was evaluated separately, the National Research Council and others have recently completed assessments of the overall lessons learned (Betsey, Hollister, and Papageorgiou, 1985; Borus, 1984; Hahn and Lerman, 1985; Manpower Demonstration Research Corporation, n.d.). In general, program managers found youth dropouts difficult to recruit and serve. Many of the strategies for basic-skills remediation and employment preparation failed to improve the employability and economic status of youth dropouts. Specifically, while a program may have succeeded in encouraging youth dropouts to return to school, it was not successful in getting them to complete their high school education or obtain their GED. Moreover, the temporary jobs did not lead to long-term gains in postprogram employment and earnings for the youth dropouts.

Even requiring youth to be enrolled in school in order to qualify for a subsidized job did not promote continuous school attendance. While having a part-time minimum-wage job did not actually reduce attendance, it was an insufficient incentive to keep dropouts in school long enough to graduate. The poor educational gains were attributable to the lack of specific remediation strategies for improving the students' basic skills. The findings suggest that strongly emphasizing GED training can increase educational attainment for out-of-school youth and that summer youth employment programs should be restructured to include basic-skills remediation and other skills training.

Reviews of the outcomes of these and other program strategies suggest that youth dropouts may need more job readiness
training and support services as part of an overall program (Berlin and Duhl, 1984; Committee for Economic Development,
1985; Education Commission of the States, 1985; McCarthy,
1985; National Governors' Association, 1985). Work experience, while critical, is not enough to meet the employment
needs of these youth or to encourage them to return to school
long enough to graduate.

Program Responsibility

No single service system has the primary responsibility
for serving the youth dropout population. This is in part because it is unclear where the responsibility lies, and in part because no single system can meet all of a community's youth
dropout needs.

It is often presumed that the schools are primarily responsible for dropout prevention and service. But it is also
argued that the schools have failed this population and thus
should not be expected to serve them. From the review of the
characteristics of youth dropouts and their reasons for leaving
school, it can be concluded that there are things schools can do
to encourage more students to stay and graduate. There are also
students at risk of dropping out because of problems outside the
school system who require resources the schools do not have.

Regardless of these points, three kinds of service agencies
commonly serve youth dropouts and those at risk of dropping
out: schools, employment and training programs, and community agencies. Public education systems, however, lack the resources to prevent more students from dropping out and can
rarely focus attention on recovering those who have left. Although youth dropouts are a targeted group for federal and
other publicly funded job training programs through which
they can get training and job placement, they are not a high
priority, because their educational deficits make them expensive
to serve. Finally, community agencies can offer supportive services but are typically limited in their scope.

Only through collaborative efforts by school systems, employment and training programs, and other public and private agencies' service systems can the need for services be comprehensively addressed within communities. Such planning and service delivery must take into account the diverse needs of potential and actual dropouts and the various program strategies that are appropriate.

Program Framework

The existing general approaches to serving dropout-prone youth demonstrate necessary and ideal core features of service delivery, instructional content, and staffing and organization. A program ought to be kept small for several reasons: smallness facilitates an intimate and supportive environment for students and a collegial relationship among the staff, and it keeps effort focused on dropout prevention. Instruction should include skill remediation, employment preparation, and job training to assist students both in graduating from high school and in preparing for post–high school employment. Academic classroom instruction should be mixed with experiential learning to motivate students and to reinforce both types of learning. A program should be structured to help students cope with problems that are barriers to their education, either by serving them directly or by referring them elsewhere.

Resolving the dropout problem requires more than the addition of miniprograms for a select group of students with academic and personal problems. As the National Coalition of Advocates for Students has recommended, the delivery of education in general must be reviewed to improve all students' chances for maximum educational attainment and to prevent the need for more dropout prevention services later. This suggests that a two-pronged approach, combining specific programs with a revamping of all curricula and instruction, is most appropriate for reducing the dropout rate.

Based on this review of the scope of the youth dropout problem, the kinds of services available, and policy and program recommendations on what is needed, we have devised a program planning framework that encompasses a range of targeted approaches. This framework classifies students into four groups according to the causes and likelihood of their dropping out:

1. The first group consists of students who are still in school, but who are marginally at risk of dropping out. They are still motivated to graduate from high school, but their low grades and lack of post–high school plans make them candidates for dropping out.
2. The second group consists of those who are interested in staying in school but cannot because of personal circumstances, such as the need to work or the responsibilities of parenthood.
3. The third group consists of students who are at great risk of dropping out, as evidenced by their lack of interest, poor attendance, and poor academic performance.
4. The final group consists of those who have already left school but need services to complete their education and thus be better prepared for employment. Returning to high school is probably not an option, but obtaining basic-skills training and preparing for the GED are.

The framework also incorporates a two-pronged approach, focusing both on programs that address individual needs, as outlined above, and on the entire dropout problem as it faces school districts and communities. Programs are arranged in a progression of service strategies and program organization from the simplest to most complex. The six categories of programs and services are described below.

Supplemental Services. The first type of program is one in which supportive counseling and job readiness preparation are provided to marginally performing students who are still in school. While these programs are limited in scope, they can be sufficient to encourage some dropout-prone students to complete high school. Programs of this type are best for youth who are likely to drop out because they are uninvolved in school activities, have poor opinions of themselves, or lack post–high school plans. Support groups and part-time employment are inexpensive ways to assist these youth. These programs can easily be sponsored by organizations external to the school or integrated with an existing educational program.

Removal of Barriers to Continued Education. The second group of programs is designed for youth whose economic, family, or personal responsibilities keep them out of school. These programs are structured to help students cope with their competing responsibilities and provide a way for them to complete high school. For example, a school-based day-care center permits teenage mothers to continue with their high school course work. Such programs, because of their attention to external problems, can often be funded through state and federal sources specifically designed for these support services.

Comprehensive School-Affiliated Programs. The third group is made up of comprehensive programs for students who are likely to drop out because of serious academic and attendance problems. These programs often combine an array of education, employment preparation, and counseling services for potential dropouts in a comprehensive, multiservice approach that encourages students to remain in school. They are designed to address intensively early manifestations of academic and attendance problems. These programs can often use private-sector resources for program content and funding.

Services for Out-of-School Youth. The fourth category consists of comprehensive programs for students who have already dropped out. They offer a menu of services to be combined in one program to address the many problems facing young dropouts. The assumption behind these programs is that it is unrealistic to assume that many students who quit school will later reenter. They focus on helping youth to achieve basic skills and to obtain the GED, while also helping them to prepare for employment.

School Systemwide Approaches. The fifth type of program combines targeted and general strategies to increase the number of students who stay in school and graduate. This ap-

proach acknowledges the school system's responsibility to prevent substantial percentages of students from dropping out.
Alternative programs for students at risk of dropping out are
combined with consideration of ways to restructure the schools
to respond better to students' varied educational needs.

Citywide Approaches. The sixth type goes beyond the
school systemwide approach to encompass the larger community or city. This approach draws on the resources of businesses,
universities, and other social agencies. It assumes that dropping
out is more than the school system's problem. Like the school
systemwide approaches, this approach reflects the idea that
the problems that cause students to drop out actually affect a
much larger group of students than the dropouts themselves.
This realization has stimulated interest in improving the organization of schooling and the incorporation of community services; as a result, it has improved a city's and a school system's
ability to retain a greater portion of its student population.

Program Illustrations of the Framework

In the chapters that follow are fourteen case summaries
of programs and strategies aimed at redirecting potential and actual youth dropouts toward completing their education and preparing for employment. The examples were selected to illustrate
the range of possible approaches that can work to help potential
dropouts, students who would not attend school without support services, and youth already out of school who would like
to complete their high school education. Some illustrate attempts to revamp a school's or a school system's delivery of
education in order to improve its retention of students. The
various approaches are presented in order from the simplest in
scope and purpose to the most complex in the mixture of services and collaborating interests. How these programs were identified and documented is summarized in Appendix A.

The fourteen programs and strategies were selected to
show different ways in which services can be combined and delivered, how various funding sources can be utilized, and how

service partnerships can be formed between schools and community groups to address a local school dropout problem. Some have been well tested and represent proven practices. Others represent promising efforts but are either too new or lack evaluative information to demonstrate their effectiveness. Nonetheless, together they represent a wide range of strategies and approaches for improving the educational achievement and employment opportunities for dropouts and dropout-prone youth. While our priority was to illustrate this variety, several methodological and programmatic considerations helped us narrow and refine the selection.

The first consideration for inclusion was the quality and creativity of the combination of services and resources. The complicated and often interrelated problems associated with dropping out of school call for many services to be delivered in one program. Because funding has become increasingly limited, the creation of new programs has become more dependent on less traditional funding sources. The selected programs illustrate different ways of funding and delivering services—for example, by forming interagency partnerships or by combining separately funded services into a comprehensive program.

A second consideration was the replicability of the programs and strategies. The program elements could not have been designed so specifically for one site that they were not capable of being adapted in part or as a whole elsewhere. With few exceptions, we also selected programs that had been in place more than two years. Moreover, every attempt was made to document the effectiveness of the program strategies. Unless the funding source required it, however, programs often lacked even limited evaluation information. The reader is cautioned whenever such information is unavailable.

The third consideration was to represent a cross-section of the regions and demographics of the United States. Programs were selected primarily from urban areas, where the school dropout problem is most severe. Several states and cities have been experimenting with dropout prevention and service efforts much longer than others. We invariably found several that met our criteria clustered in one area; this is why our selections occasionally include two different programs from one city or state.

The final consideration was of program design and administration. Regardless of the focus of individual programs, the targeted youth have a wide range of problems that can limit a program's success. Therefore, we selected programs that incorporated multiple services, paying particular attention to basic-skill development, employment preparation, support services, and self-esteem development. In addition, on the assumption that the continued operation of programs required a broad base of support and funding, we selected programs that drew upon resources from a number of agencies and interested parties.

Using the Summaries

Each chapter begins with a discussion of the importance and the unique features of each program. The program summaries themselves cover the approach, context and history, curriculum and operations, students served, staffing and administration, funding, and demonstrated effectiveness of each program.

These in-depth summaries are presented to give policy makers, educators, program planners, and the interested public a sense of the context, operations, and financial and administrative support that make up each approach. The summaries thus offer some insight into what ought to be considered in adapting or incorporating a program. For those who want to know more about a program, names of persons to contact for further information are listed in Appendix C.

Table of Programs

1. Supplemental Services
    Twelve-Together
    Adopt-a-Student
    Summer Youth Employment Program
2. Programs to Remove the Barriers to Continued Education
    Secondary Credit Exchange Program
    Murray-Wright High School Day-Care Center
    Adolescent Primary Health Care Clinic

3. Comprehensive School-Affiliated Programs
   Job Readiness Program
   Project COFFEE
   Rich's Academy
4. Services for Out-of-School Youth
   Alternative Schools Network
   Educational Clinics
5. School Systemwide Approaches
   Systemic Approach to Dropout Prevention
   Dropout Prevention and Recovery Program
6. Citywide Approach
   Boston Compact

3

Supplemental Services for Potential Dropouts: Providing Supportive Counseling and Positive Role Models

Sample surveys have shown that youth dropouts, far more than their peers who remain in and graduate from high school, feel that teachers do not care about them. Youth dropouts are far less likely to be involved in school activities and generally have a poorer opinion of themselves and their ability than their in-school peers. It is not possible to determine how much these feelings contribute to a student's decision to leave school without graduating, but supplemental support programs that address these feelings have been shown to be effective in helping students remain in school. Also effective are programs that offer youth a chance to experience the world of work and thereby develop a more realistic appreciation of the benefits of earning a high school diploma.

Community agencies and business groups interested in encouraging students to complete their education are well suited to devising support service programs. They can more easily recruit adults to serve as role models and provide or solicit part-time and summer jobs. Moreover, support groups and part-time employment are inexpensive ways of assisting dropout-prone youth and are particularly effective for those who may just feel directionless.

Programs that offer youth exposure to the realities of work can encourage more students to stay in school. By designing a program that maximizes the educational lessons learned in the workplace, an employment and training agency can extend the benefits of part-time work into dropout prevention.

The three program summaries that follow illustrate different kinds of supplemental service programs. They show how interested groups can use limited resources and voluntary assistance to help potential dropouts think about their future, plan for employment, and learn to cope with their academic and personal problems.

The first is Twelve-Together, sponsored by the Metropolitan Detroit Youth Foundation (MDYF), a private, nonprofit youth agency. The program uses peer groups to help potential dropouts find constructive ways to cope with their personal and academic problems and to encourage them to remain in school. Volunteer adult group leaders and students in the peer group who are not at risk of dropping out provide two kinds of role models for the potential dropouts.

The second program is Adopt-a-Student, jointly sponsored by a business personnel professionals' association and the public school system of Atlanta. Low-achieving high school juniors and seniors are paired with volunteer business people who serve as their mentors. Through the close support and availability of adult role models, youth are encouraged to plan concretely for their lives after high school.

The third program is the New Bedford Summer Youth Employment Program, a summer jobs program for economically disadvantaged young people. The program builds work-related learning and basic-skills remediation into summer job experiences in the public and private sectors.

Most participants targeted for the programs lack post-high school plans. Appropriately, all three programs offer job readiness workshops, giving students practical lessons in how to think about and apply for jobs. The programs also illustrate ways to encourage businesses to contribute staff volunteers, services, and resources to extend the scope of the programs.

TWELVE-TOGETHER
Detroit, Michigan

Twelve-Together is a community-based program that organizes groups of twelve ninth graders in each of the twenty Detroit high schools into weekly peer-counseling sessions. Six poorly achieving students and six successful students are selected for each peer group. With the assistance of two adult volunteers, the students learn to express their personal and educational problems and find appropriate solutions. The program is based on the theory that positive peer pressure can help teenagers deal effectively with their own problems and support one another. Peer-group counseling is believed to be helpful in reducing the stresses that inhibit young people's ability to stay in school, increasing students' belief in themselves and their abilities, and providing positive reinforcement to their desire to graduate. In the trusting atmosphere of the peer group, youth can help each other to understand and solve their problems, to develop and articulate their goals, and to attend and complete school.

By using volunteer peer-group advisers and contributed space, the program, run by the Metropolitan Detroit Youth Foundation (MDYF), operates as a low-cost counseling program for dropout prevention. Begun in 1982, the program is now seeing its first participants graduate from high school. As the program has evolved and its design and operations have been improved, participating students have done better in comparisons with nonparticipating students. The program is supported by foundation grants and corporate gifts. A federal grant will permit substantial program expansion in 1986–87.

Background

Like many urban public school systems in the United States, the Detroit schools have a high annual dropout rate. In 1984–85, the system reported that 13.8 percent of high school students dropped out each year, representing a cumulative 45 percent dropout rate for entering ninth-grade students. In 1983, a group of educators and community leaders formed the High School Dropout Prevention Network of Southeast Michigan, which the MDYF cosponsors. The network has drawn substantial public attention to Detroit's dropout rate and the need for more services.

At the same time, the MDYF began addressing Detroit's dropout problem through its special projects. The MDYF was established in 1967 as a private, nonprofit advocacy group intended to make Detroit's major institutions more responsive to youth and their needs. It has operated several youth programs, many in cooperation with the Detroit public schools. Currently, it runs clerical and computer skills training programs, a college preparatory basic-skills program, a peer-support program for eleventh graders in cooperation with the Chrysler Corporation, and Twelve-Together.

The MDYF first tried peer counseling in a federally funded pilot project called Project Graduate, which ran during the summer of 1981. The program provided leadership training and tutoring for sixty high school dropouts, thirty of whom also received peer counseling. The increased benefits for those in peer counseling convinced the MDYF of this method's success in working with youth.

On the basis of this experience, the MDYF designed Twelve-Together, adapting Project Graduate to a dropout prevention program. They targeted in-school ninth graders, assuming that students were most likely to drop out at that grade. The staff spent the summer obtaining the approval of and making arrangements with the school system and recruiting and training volunteer group advisers. A Detroit public school teacher trained the staff in peer-counseling techniques. By the fall of 1982, the MDYF was ready to begin the first year of Twelve-Together.

From the beginning, the program has received substantial funding from the Charles Stewart Mott Foundation as well as a mixture of small foundation grants and charitable gifts. In 1983, businesses and companies began to sponsor groups, providing extra in-kind support and resources.

Description

The program begins during the summer, when the MDYF staff recruit adult volunteer advisers to work with peer groups during the school year. The MDYF advertises for volunteers through the media and flyers, but it also recruits many through friends, churches, and the MDYF's business contacts. Recently, many employees of sponsoring companies have volunteered to be advisers.

Beginning in the early fall, MDYF staff visit each of the twenty Detroit high schools over a five-month period to recruit student participants. Through prior arrangements made with Detroit public school officials and each school's administration, staff members meet with all ninth graders in assemblies or separate classes. There, the staff explain the program and the requirements for participation. Interested students sign up after school and are interviewed by the staff.

The MDYF staff try to choose a mix of students for each peer group, selecting six students who are doing well in school and six whose personal and academic characteristics indicate that they are at risk of dropping out. According to program staff, from 100 to 150 students apply to Twelve-Together from each school. The staff invite to join the program those who have set goals for themselves and are committed to staying in school.

All students must have written parental permission to participate in the program. Occasionally, parents are reluctant; in some cases, staff will meet with parents to explain the program and to encourage them to allow their child's participation.

The first step in participation is to attend a retreat. Each month for five months the students recruited from four high schools and the eight assigned adult advisers go on a weekend retreat at a rural lodge. During the retreat, the students and advisers participate in several group activities to develop relationships and to foster rapport. Students pledge to themselves and each other to fulfill the program steps: to study for an average of one and one-half hours daily and to participate in a minimum of thirty meetings, including twenty-two peer-group sessions, the retreat, a parent reception, and six Saturday afternoon academic forums. Students are to pay $15 to cover retreat expenses. Those who cannot afford the fee (about 25 percent) are given a "scholarship" by the MDYF.

A week after the retreat, Twelve-Together staff invite the students and their parents to a reception. There, parents learn about the program and about what is expected of their children. They are given suggestions on how to help support the program and their children's progress in school and are made aware of each student's commitment to studying and attending the meetings. Parents and students are complimented for their success in life so far and encouraged to work together to make it to graduation.

At the reception, group advisers meet the parents and, if possible, arrange to visit their homes. The home visits give the advisers a chance to get to know the parents and students in their family environment, to involve the parents further in encouraging their children, and to build a trusting relationship with the families.

Following the reception, the peer groups begin meeting weekly for two-hour sessions after school. Students and advisers are given a structure and rules with which to run each meeting. Advisers open the meetings by reviewing the student problem discussed the previous week, the solutions suggested, and the progress made. Then the students, sitting in a circle, take turns describing a problem they face and identifying it as one of twelve problem areas outlined in the program guide. The problems are characterized as follows: is inconsiderate of self and others; has poor self-image; has communication problems; is immature; loses temper easily; has authority problems; has alcohol or drug abuse problems; lies; is a negative leader; is a negative follower; provokes others; and is lazy.

By majority vote, one student's problem is picked for discussion. After more detailed description and questions and answers, the group members suggest ways for the student to solve the difficulty. Throughout the meeting, advisers help the discussion along by asking questions, but not by offering opinions. At the end of the meeting, the advisers review what has taken place and comment on the suggestions, on how well the meeting went, and on each student's involvement. According to the advisers, the peer-counseling sessions focus equally on discussions of school, family, and personal problems. Most advisers report that they use the problem identification guide to structure the peer-group meetings and discussions.

It is impressed upon the students and advisers that for the peer-group structure to be successful, confidentiality must be maintained. If a problem arises that requires outside intervention, the advisers consult with the MDYF staff and encourage the student involved to take appropriate action.

As part of their participation in Twelve-Together, the students must attend six Saturday morning academic forums, sponsored monthly by the MDYF at a centrally located church conference center. During the forums, staff bring in speakers and work with the students to improve their motivational skills. Former Twelve-Together students are invited to attend these forums as well.

Students may also go to the MDYF center for tutoring. In 1985, the MDYF began using the Comprehensive Competencies Program, a computerized basic-skills training program. The center also has volunteers to help students in problem subject areas.

Finally, as part of their participation in Twelve-Together, the students must promise to study for one and one-half hours every night. During the peer-group meetings, the groups review how well students have done in meeting this objective. Students must also share their report cards in the meetings.

When the students finish the program at the end of ninth grade, the program staff encourage them to continue to support each other as a group throughout the remainder of high school.

In the program's fourth year, the staff experimented with substituting required tutoring for the academic forums. Dissatisfied with the results, they changed the program back to optional tutoring and monthly academic forums. At the same time, a federal grant allowed them to expand the program substantially; they are adding twenty-two new groups in Detroit, for a total of forty-two groups. They also hope to interest organizations outside Detroit and Michigan in starting Twelve-Together groups. As a result, more program staff have been added to share in the recruiting and monitoring responsibilities.

Participants

The program targets ninth graders in the twenty Detroit public high schools and serves up to twelve students in each school. To participate, students must express a genuine desire to overcome the obstacles between them and high school graduation. They must be willing to commit themselves to the requirements detailed above. Half the students selected must be at risk of dropping out of school—that is, they must meet at least two of the MDYF's four criteria: being sixteen or older; having had *D*'s or *F*'s in two or more courses the previous year; having been absent twenty or more days in the previous semester; or living with only one parent. The counseling aspect of the program interests both potential dropouts and other students, so there is little difficulty in recruiting a balanced mix of participants.

After the initial recruitment and interviewing, which is done on a school-by-school basis, the staff invite from eighteen to twenty students per school (about 360–400 students in all) to join the program and come on the retreat. Eleven or twelve students from each school (about 220–240 students in all) eventually come on the retreat and make the program pledge. The staff try to recruit equal numbers of boys and girls, although they find that girls are more likely to volunteer. Once in the program, boys and girls are equally likely to participate actively.

The program's pledge and structure emphasize good attendance and responsible behavior. If students are absent from any of the thirty required meetings with a valid excuse, they can make up the session by doing a task selected by the others in the group (such as doing extra schoolwork or tutoring another member of the group), or, if the group agrees, all members can attend a make-up meeting. Program staff try to impress upon the students that being absent is inconsiderate of the others because of their commitment to supporting one another.

To foster intragroup reliance and support, the program staff emphasize that an individual's success in the program depends on all students in the group doing well. The group advisers try to encourage the participating students to bring poorly attending students back into the group. Yet this is not always possible and students do drop out or attend irregularly. The re-

maining group members must convince their advisers that they
have done everything in their power to bring the dropout member back. A follow-up of six Twelve-Together groups in 1985–
86 showed that 67 percent of the seventy-two students completed all Twelve-Together requirements; 75 percent attended at
least 40 percent of the meetings.

While the program emphasizes group success, the staff re-
ward individual as well as group efforts at a program graduation
ceremony in June. Groups and individuals are recognized for having met all program requirements. Even those who stayed with the
program but did not meet all requirements receive an award. Students who have perfect attendance, who are passing into the tenth
grade, and who showed the most improvement in grades and in
group participation are also recognized during the ceremony. In
1985–86, seventeen of the twenty groups were recognized for
meeting all program requirements. About 400–450 students,
parents, and other relatives attended the graduation ceremony.

In 1984–85, Twelve-Together enrolled 223 students. Ten
schools had groups consisting of equal numbers of potential
dropouts and other students; five schools had groups in which
potential dropouts predominated; and five schools had the reverse. Of those who initially enrolled, 14 percent, or thirty-two
students, later left the program. Most did so because of a lack of
interest (35 percent), because their parents removed them from
the group (25 percent), or because of other reasons, such as
moving or scheduling conflicts. Of the 190 students who remained in the program, 55 percent were potential dropouts.

A Detroit public schools graduation requirement encourages the students to participate fully in the program. All Detroit
high school students must accumulate 200 hours of work experience to graduate from high school. One credit for work experience is earned for every twenty hours spent in Twelve-
Together activities; students average from two to five credits for
their participation in the program.

Staffing and Administration

In 1985–86, the program was directed by two MDYF
staff members; one was responsible for recruiting and selecting

youth participants, the other for recruiting and training advisers. Both ran the weekend retreats and tracked each group's progress. Another part-time staff member ran the tutoring program, which was open to both Twelve-Together students and others.

Forty advisers were recruited to work in pairs with each of the twenty groups. Advisers were selected on the basis of their ability to express themselves easily and to handle sensitive topics, such as sex and drugs, without being judgmental. Male adult volunteers were more difficult to recruit than females; in 1985-86, only fourteen of the forty advisers were male. Program staff made their expectations for responsible attendance and role model behavior clear to the advisers from the beginning; advisers who were irresponsible were replaced.

Each adviser attended a day-long volunteer training session during the summer. There they learned how to conduct peer-group meetings and to work with the list of problem categories they were to use. Another session was held before the retreat. The advisers met each month as a group with an MDYF staff person to discuss problems with their peer groups and to share ideas and solutions. An MDYF staff member visited each group at least twice during the year and more frequently as needed to observe and follow up on an adviser's performance.

While the staff prefer that advisers stay with the program for more than one year, this is not always feasible. Only fifteen of the forty advisers in 1985-86 had worked with groups the year before. Some advisers do not continue because of personal or professional constraints, because they find that running peer groups involves more responsibility than they had expected, or because they are not invited back.

The Detroit public school system has supported the Twelve-Together program from its inception, primarily through collaboration and allocation of space. The superintendent directs the principals of all high schools to cooperate with MDYF staff each year. In turn, each school's head of guidance or another staff person makes arrangements for student recruiting and interviewing and works with MDYF staff to coordinate the program. To keep the public school officials abreast of the program's progress, MDYF staff make periodic reports to the board of education and area superintendents.

In 1983, the MDYF began recruiting businesses to "adopt" groups, asking them to provide resources such as space for meetings, refreshments and token incentives, and funds to cover the cost of the retreats. Blue Cross/Blue Shield was the first company to volunteer. Program staff found that the added incentives and exposure to business helped to keep students involved and motivated. Since then, MDYF staff have actively pursued corporate sponsorship of groups; in 1986, fourteen groups were adopted by fourteen companies.

Funding

The program costs consist primarily of supervisory staff salaries and retreat expenses. Other operating resources are contributed and the advisers' time is volunteered. The public schools and various companies contribute space, and some companies also provide token incentives for the students, such as T-shirts or field trips.

The total program budget in 1985–86 was $110,000, serving 240 students at an average cost of $458 per student. A Charles Stewart Mott Foundation grant provides $50,000 per year; the remainder comes from a mixture of foundation grants, gifts, and personal contributions. As the program expands, the per-student costs should decrease, since additional program staff will not be needed. The MDYF has begun asking companies to sponsor a new group with a $3,000 donation.

Evaluation

An evaluation of the program and the participants' academic and attendance improvement shows that the program has been increasingly successful during its first three years of operation. Overall, students showed gains in self-esteem, motivation, and problem-solving and interpersonal skills. In 1985–86, 67 percent of the students participating in Twelve-Together attended thirty meetings and studied at least an average of one and one-half hours per day, just below the MDYF's goal of 75 percent.

More important, the more students became involved in the program, the better their academic performance. The MDYF contracted with an outside evaluation team to review the program and the students' progress for the first three years. The 1985 evaluation compared the performance of participants who had attended at least 40 percent of the meetings with non-participating students from the same class. First-year participants, who were by then in the eleventh grade, were earning the same number of credits as the comparison group. Evaluators and program staff thought the lack of any difference was attributable to start-up problems and difficulties in forming the control groups.

Second- and third-year participants, however, showed dramatic increases in credit accumulation. The third-year participants were 55 percent more likely than the comparison group to earn enough credits to be promoted into the tenth grade, and second-year students were 28 percent more likely to earn enough credits to be promoted into the eleventh grade.

In the spring of 1985, the evaluation team surveyed or had the advisers telephone 94 percent of the Twelve-Together students. The team also surveyed at least one adviser from each group. Eighty-eight percent of the students rated the program good or better, as did 97 percent of the advisers. Seventy-seven percent of the students and 82 percent of the advisers rated the peer-counseling sessions good or better. Of the other activities, the retreat was rated highest and the academic forums lowest, although more than half the students liked the forums. Most of the participants thought they and other students in the group were benefiting from Twelve-Together. Substantial proportions of student respondents thought that the program would greatly help other students stay in school (47 percent), get better grades (37 percent), resolve personal problems (40 percent), and attend school more regularly (28 percent).

About fourteen of the twenty group advisers interviewed for an evaluation of the program reported that they had extensive contact with most of their students' parents throughout the year. Seven of the twenty advisers reported that parents were very positive and supportive; three reported having problems; the remaining advisers reported limited or no problems.

Peer counseling appears to be an effective way of providing youth with support and helping them to build self-esteem. While it is currently beyond the funding and staff capacity of the MDYF to continue the groups beyond the ninth grade, the evaluation findings and student comments seem to indicate a need for this. Several past participants in Twelve-Together suggested that it would be useful for the program to continue the meetings throughout all four years of high school, particularly to encourage students academically.

The basic program components of Twelve-Together are easily replicated, assuming that cooperation of the local school system can be obtained and volunteers recruited. The MDYF staff have prepared a detailed professional guide on running peer-group counseling programs for other organizations that are interested in starting one. They receive frequent requests for information on the program and currently are helping two Michigan communities begin similar programs.

Twelve-Together

Program Components

- Supplemental counseling program, focusing on problem solving and academics
- Peer-group meetings
- Student pledge to participate and to study one and one-half hours each day
- Volunteer adult advisers
- Cooperation between school district and community organizations

Program Inputs and Outcomes

- Target population: Twelve high- and low-risk ninth graders in each of twenty high schools
- Costs: $460 per student; contributed space
- Outcomes: Improved attendance and academic performance

ADOPT-A-STUDENT
Atlanta, Georgia

The Adopt-a-Student program pairs business volunteers ("consultants") as mentors or "big brothers/sisters" with low-achieving high school juniors and seniors. Through a relationship with a consultant and monthly job preparation workshops, students are encouraged to finish high school and to develop post–high school career plans. The program is jointly run by the Atlanta public schools and the Merit Employment Association (MEA).

In 1982, Atlanta school officials appealed to the MEA, an association of personnel professionals, to devise a motivational program for students who are in the bottom quarter of their class and have few or no post–high school plans. Without assistance, these students might not complete high school; if they did, they would be ill-prepared for employment. In response, the MEA designed and sponsored the Adopt-a-Student program in cooperation with the Atlanta public schools. The school system contributes the personnel necessary to select and supervise the student participants, donates space for meetings, and coordinates the program with the MEA. The MEA's members volunteer their time as consultants, coordinators, and planners and, if necessary, contribute other workshop materials. The program is strongly supported by the school system and the participating businesses, which encourage their staff to participate.

Since 1982, participation in the Adopt-a-Student program has grown from 10 student in two schools to 210 students in all Atlanta high schools. Program participants are more likely to complete high school and become employed than their non-participating counterparts.

Background

Atlanta has a large, predominantly minority school system of 71,000 students. Enrollment has declined by 21 percent over the ten years since voluntary desegregation became effective.

Attendance is good and the dropout rate low, however, in comparison to other urban areas. Approximately 24,000 students attend twenty-one high schools; the average attendance rate is 91 percent. Four percent of the students drop out each year, yielding a cumulative high school dropout rate of about 15 percent.

At the same time, Atlanta's economy is healthy and growing, with low unemployment and an expanding business sector. Yet many Atlanta public school graduates as well as dropouts are excluded from these opportunities. Nine percent of the 1985 graduates were neither employed nor in a postsecondary education program when surveyed several months after graduation. In response, the mayor and superintendent of schools mobilized public and private resources to better prepare Atlanta's youth.

Over the past six years, Atlanta's superintendent has improved the quality of school programs and raised student performance on standardized math and reading tests above the national averages. Along with several academic improvement efforts, the Atlanta school system has collaborated with interested business and community agencies on several activities that expose students to and improve their chances for various career, education, and military options. Some businesses have adopted schools or contributed to special school improvement efforts. Each high school sponsors a career day; the MEA, a professional association of business personnel and community affairs officials, organizes a "Youth Motivation Day" in all high schools, providing speakers from a range of business fields. The Mayor's Task Force on Public Education and several corporations together sponsor an annual "Dream Jamboree," hosted at the Atlanta convention center, at which ninth, tenth, and eleventh graders from all city high schools can meet over 200 exhibitors on post–high school education programs, employment opportunities, and the military. Finally, the Atlanta Private Industry Council coordinates summer jobs for eligible high school students and out-of-school youth.

In all, the education and employment opportunities for Atlanta's youth are being improved from many sides. Yet the educational and business communities recognized that a special effort was needed to help the students least likely to benefit from these opportunities.

In 1982, the superintendent of schools asked the Atlanta Partnership of Business & Education, Inc., and later the MEA, to aid the lowest-achieving students, those in the bottom quarter of their class. Initially, the MEA declined, arguing that it was too busy organizing its annual Youth Motivation Day and was uncertain about how to serve this student population. In the following year, 1982-83, the MEA agreed to pilot a mentoring project for ten students in two schools.

Through trial and error over the next three years, the MEA developed the current Adopt-a-Student program and the administrative structure necessary to coordinate a largely volunteer effort. The project's codirectors, an Atlanta public schools official and a personnel staff member from Southern Bell, have developed and refined the way students are selected and matched with volunteer consultants, the recruitment and training of consultants, the way their relationships are monitored, the content of the workshops, and the reinforcement mechanisms for the student participants. Each year, the MEA has doubled the number of schools served by the program and recruited more business volunteers. The MEA has added employment preparation workshops and experimented with and dropped a computerized training program.

As the program grew, the MEA and the Atlanta public schools developed a large volunteer committee structure to administer the program and to maintain quality in the workshops and the mentoring relationships. In 1986, the Atlanta public schools added a central office staff member to help coordination and took over responsibility for organizing the monthly workshops. The program currently serves over 200 students from all twenty-one Atlanta high schools.

In 1985, the William T. Grant Foundation, interested in the replicability of this mentoring program, funded a three-year evaluation of the program's effectiveness, to be carried out by a Georgia State University evaluation team.

Description

The program sponsors hoped that individual encouragement and support from an employed adult would help low-achieving students gain confidence and direct them toward completing high school and pursuing a career. The program consists of two parts—the consultant-student relationship and the employment preparation workshops. In order to form a steady relationship, the MEA-recruited business volunteers are encouraged to share a weekly activity with their students, anything from tutoring to attending baseball games. All consultants and students are expected to participate in monthly job preparation workshops, which cover such topics as looking for a job, presenting oneself at a job interview, and applying for a job. The mentoring relationship is focused on helping the students think about their future employment and begin taking steps to prepare for it.

Student participation in the program is voluntary. At the beginning of the school year, the central board of education sends to each school a list of eligible students, who are in the bottom quarter of the eleventh and twelfth grades. In turn, the school contact person, usually a counselor, uses his or her own judgment to identify those students who would be willing to participate and those who could benefit from the program. Some counselors also consider the student's school attendance, participation in other school activities, or need for assistance in making post–high school plans. On average, ten students are recruited for every fourteen the counselors invite. Interested students complete an application and interest list. They are then matched by interest and location with volunteer business people, who become their consultants. In all, about 210 students are enrolled.

At the same time, MEA members recruit volunteers from their companies. The volunteers also complete an interest survey and are interviewed by MEA members to determine their eligibility for the program; the immature and unreliable are eliminated. Selected volunteers participate in a half-day training program that describes what the program expects of its volunteers and prepares them for the problems in developing and maintaining a mentoring relationship.

An MEA volunteer assigned as coordinator to each school meets with the school contact person to match volunteer consultants and students. The coordinator usually meets with the school principal to reestablish ties for the school year and to schedule the annual parents' conference. At this evening meeting, parents, students, consultants, and school personnel are invited to learn about the program. Very few parents (between one and three per school) come, although most students come to meet their consultants. Most parents show their support by giving formal permission for their children to participate.

Consultants are supposed to keep a log of all phone and personal contacts they have with their students, although often such records are not kept. Consultants plan and schedule activities with their students on their own, although they can discuss problems or activities with the school coordinator. They are expected to maintain their relationship with their students until after the student has graduated and found employment or enrolled in a postsecondary program.

The consultant-student relationship can be difficult to foster. As a result, these relationships have varied from only weekly telephone calls and joint attendance of the monthly meetings to weekly activities and tutoring, with students initiating as much interaction as the consultants. Consultants have found that shy or unmotivated students are difficult to engage. If the relationship does not work out, the coordinator will reassign students and consultants as needed.

The consultants try to help their students identify their occupational interests and plan to obtain a job that matches them. Each month, all students and consultants attend job preparation workshops, usually conducted on Saturday mornings at a centrally located middle school. The workshops cover preparing for a job search, obtaining skills and training, finding a job, and going through an interview and application. They are designed by MEA volunteers, who invite the speakers and prepare materials for a series of topics. Consultants provide other world-of-work exposure by taking students for a tour of their workplaces, discussing their own career paths, and helping their students obtain career-related materials. Finally, the Atlanta Private Industry Council helps by referring students to full-time or part-time job opportunities.

Many of the targeted students belong to few other school organizations, if any. While most need continual prodding to come to the monthly meetings and to follow through with their consultants, the majority attend the workshops and participate in the activities. It helps that the consultants and coordinators provide transportation.

Participants

All of the 2,200 high school juniors and seniors (100 per school) in the bottom quarter of their class are eligible for the program, although not all are asked to participate. These students usually have less than a 2.0 average (on a four-point scale) and may have been held back at least one year in school. From this group, counselors target students who are not handicapped, who have no post–high school plans, and who they think would benefit from the program. In all, only ten students are served in each of the twenty-one high schools. Of 250–300 students solicited for program participation in 1985–86, 210 enrolled.

In 1985–86, program staff decided to solicit equal numbers of juniors and seniors, five of each from each school; of those who eventually enrolled, 61 percent were seniors. In addition, 95 percent of the participating students were black, and about 50 percent were male. Sixty-five percent of the students were enrolled in their school's free or reduced-price lunch program and 69 percent were living in female-headed families. Thirty-two percent of the participants maintained part-time jobs during the school year.

To complete the program successfully, students must attend at least 70 percent of the workshops. Attendance is encouraged with door prizes and competitions among the schools for the best attendance all year. At the end of the school year, students with the best overall attendance and best achievement receive a certificate at the program's awards night. Students who have satisfactorily participated in the program receive certificates at their school's awards assembly. There are no penalties for poor attendance, although students who show a lack of interest or involvement are dropped from the program by a joint decision of the program staff.

During the school year, about fifty students dropped out of the program because of lack of interest or other circumstances, although the program volunteers made an attempt to contact the students and encourage their participation. Of the seniors eligible to graduate in the spring of 1986, 92 percent did so; 85 percent of the juniors earned enough credits to be promoted.

Staffing and Administration

The program is jointly administered by the Atlanta public schools and the MEA; representatives from each serve as co-directors. Both rely heavily on the assistance of business volunteers to staff and to administer the program and on each school contact person to facilitate student involvement.

The Atlanta public school system, through its office of job placement, is responsible for handling student participation. It notifies the schools about the program, identifies the pool of eligible students, and follows up on student enrollment activities. It is at the school system's direction that local high schools assign coordinating responsibilities to a school contact person and make space available for meetings and monthly workshops. With the recent expansion of this program and similar efforts, the office of job placement has added a staff person to follow up on the coordinators and the workshops.

The MEA, with the continuous leadership of one volunteer from Southern Bell, has established an Adopt-a-Student committee to oversee its administration and operations. Ten consultants are assigned to a school; each is paired with one or two students. A coordinator, also a business volunteer, is assigned to each school to supervise and assist the consultants. Coordinators are usually selected from among seasoned consultants. In addition to overseeing their assigned school, they must prepare progress reports and year-end program reports. Each co-ordinator holds regular meetings for consultants and meets with other coordinators and the MEA codirector for training, planning, and administrative activities.

Just as some students do not participate adequately in the program, neither do some volunteer consultants. Despite the screening and training, about two consultants in ten either drop out of the program or are found to be unsuitable.

As the program expands, the MEA and the office of job placement continue to revise its structure and content. In 1985-86, the MEA Adopt-a-Student committee divided into subcommittees on the workshop curriculum, participant handbooks, business volunteer recruitment, screening, and publicity to improve program administration. Each year, the committee and codirectors establish new program objectives. For 1985-86, these included expanding the program to all high schools and involving volunteers from eleven additional companies. Both objectives were achieved.

Funding

In addition to the Atlanta public schools' contribution of staff (for in-school coordination and office of job placement direction), the Adopt-a-Student program is supported by volunteers' time and in-kind contributions. The school system contributes space for the meetings. Members of the MEA solicit contributions from local businesses, amounting to about $10,000 annually, for workshop refreshments, door and attendance prizes, and workshop materials.

Evaluation

Throughout the program's existence, program staff have monitored student participation and postgraduation activities. They have assessed the usefulness of various program features and changed them as needed. Students periodically complete evaluation surveys rating workshop topics.

The program codirectors and the MEA have planned several changes for 1986-87. First, rather than enroll both eleventh and twelfth graders, they will now enroll only eleventh graders. Second, the program will last for eighteen months, beginning in the second semester of the junior year and continuing through the senior year. The first six months will allow time for the student-consultant relationship to develop. The program codirectors have determined that the relationship and its benefits for self-esteem development are the most critical components of the program and therefore should be emphasized. Finally, they hope to expand the program to serve 1,000 students in all high schools.

In addition to internal process evaluation measures, the William T. Grant Foundation, because of its interest in action research and mentoring programs, has funded researchers at Georgia State University to evaluate the program's impact. For this three-year study, the researchers are tracking 300 participating and comparison-group students, 100 consultants, and 10 coordinators selected from 10 schools.

Evaluators surveyed half the students from the 1985–86 program year and found that 75 percent of the eighty-eight students rated the program highly. Not surprisingly, those that rated the program highly were far more likely to see their consultants often and to consider the consultant a friend. In all, 32 percent of the students reported seeing their consultant three or more times a month. Sixty-eight percent spent time with their consultant at workshops and 60 percent at their own homes. Sixty-four percent viewed their consultant as a friend, and only 17 percent viewed their relationship as unfriendly. Between 63 and 78 percent of the students reported that they could reach their consultants when needed and that they and the consultants returned each other's phone calls and talked about improving grades and getting a job after graduation. About 63 percent of the students said their parents were interested in the program and liked their consultants.

The evaluators followed up eighty-eight students from the 1984–85 program six months after graduation. While 61 percent of these students were employed or enrolled in a post-secondary program immediately after graduation, 93 percent were so occupied six months later.

For the 1985–86 school year, the evaluators compared

the ninety-six participants from ten randomly selected schools with a comparison group of sixty-one students whom counselors had nominated for the program but, for the purpose of the evaluation, had never invited to join. At the end of the school year, the participants had done slightly better than the comparison students in their attendance rate (82 versus 79 percent) and grade point average (1.70 versus 1.65). Greater differences were found in the percentage of juniors who were promoted (85 percent of the participants versus 80 percent of the comparison group) and the percentage of seniors who graduated (92 versus 84 percent). The number of students who dropped out of school was unavailable.

The consultant's relationship with the student is the most critical and influential component of the program; it depends on good matches of personality and interests and the follow-through efforts of the volunteer consultants. About one-third of the relationships do not work out: either the student or the consultant cannot or will not be involved. In the better relationships, the pair spend more than the minimum amount of time together and visit each other's homes so that the consultant gets to know the student's family and the student is included in the consultant's family. Program staff observed that parental support and encouragement make a big difference in how well a student does in the program.

Because of the critical influence of these relationships, changes are being made in the program's design to improve mentor-student compatibility. Consultants will be matched with students when they are juniors and will maintain a mentoring relationship for eighteen months. Fewer workshops will be scheduled, and those that are held will pay more attention to developing student's self-esteem.

The Adopt-a-Student program provides a unique career-oriented support system for low-achieving high school eleventh and twelfth graders. To some extent, the program's success can be attributed to each student's willingness to participate and motivation to succeed. The evaluation findings showed that similar nonparticipating students did less well academically and in completing school, suggesting that the mentoring of business volunteers does help. The program staff hope that the long-term influence on career paths will be as positive as the short-term effects. The program is unusual, too, in the role taken by the MEA. While professional personnel associations are not uncommon in many cities, it is rare for such groups to address actively the employment preparation needs of in-school youth. Here, the MEA has lent its expertise in a very useful way.

The program has received national attention through presentations at professional meetings. As a result, many communities have made inquiries about replicating the program.

Adopt-a-Student

Program Components

- Supplemental program, focusing on post–high school plans
- Business volunteers as mentors
- Monthly job preparation workshops
- Weekly consultant-student activities
- Job-search support after graduation
- Business and school collaboration

Program Inputs and Outcomes

- Target population: 210 students from all 21 Atlanta public high schools, from the bottom 25 percent of the class
- Costs: Volunteer time from business employees; public school space; Atlanta public schools administration
- Outcomes: 92 percent high school graduation rate; 93 percent job placement or postsecondary education enrollment rate

SUMMER YOUTH EMPLOYMENT PROGRAM
New Bedford, Massachusetts

To provide youth with a range of vocational experiences and educational support along with summer employment opportunities is the objective of the summer jobs program of the New Bedford Private Industry Council (PIC), through the Office for Job Partnerships (OJP). To this end, the OJP has developed private- and public-sector summer jobs that require different levels of skills; some involve related enrichment activities and supplemental academic work.

A major goal of the seven-week program is to incorporate learning into the summer work. Young people aged fourteen to twenty-one who are eligible for services funded by the Job Training Partnership Act (JTPA) are matched by skills and interests with local employers who have pledged to provide jobs and have clearly defined what the jobs will entail. About half the positions offer career exposure or related instruction along with the summer work. In all, 1,297 youth worked in a wide variety of entry-level jobs over a seven-week period in 1986.

All program participants are required to take a job readiness course; remedial instruction is available for those having academic trouble in school. The program management and the youth's salaries are funded by local JTPA monies.

Background

After several years of high unemployment and a depressed industrial base, the New Bedford area began to steadily grow in 1983. While the unemployment rate was at a low overall rate of 5.8 percent for the New Bedford–Cape Cod area by 1985, it was 14 percent among youth aged sixteen to nineteen and 11.2 percent for those aged twenty and twenty-one. As a result, the local PIC, through the OJP, a private, nonprofit employment and training agency, has focused its services on the groups with the greatest need, particularly economically disadvantaged youth, who make up 23 percent of all the disadvantaged. Because of their limited employment opportunities, school dropouts are also a target; almost 50 percent of the area's JTPA-eligible population lack a high school diploma.

Recently, the PIC has begun to address related employment problems of its target groups. Employers had complained about the lack of job readiness and basic academic skills among their young applicants. The OJP has tried to improve the employability of the disadvantaged youth it places by incorporating appropriate training into its summer youth employment program. Although the resulting program model has never been evaluated, it illustrates a method of combining world-of-work exposure and academic learning in a summer employment program.

Description

The OJP's Summer Youth Employment Program has four objectives. The first is to expand the vocational horizons of JTPA-eligible youth by making them aware of the job opportunities in the community. The second is to upgrade their basic skills, either directly, through basic-skills remediation, or indirectly, through job-related enrichment activities that require communication, writing, and computational skills. The third is to reinforce good work habits through the employers' and program counselors' supervision. The fourth is to provide JTPA-eligible youth with income and, for many, their first job.

The OJP begins planning the program late in the winter. The staff sends notices to local high schools and social service agencies and places television, radio, and newspaper advertisements. Eligible youth are enrolled on a first-come, first-served basis. Those aged fourteen to seventeen must apply for a work permit; those aged fourteen and fifteen must also have a physical exam before they can be eligible for work.

After the youth have been registered with the OJP, they meet with job placement counselors who review their background, previous work experience, health, and any other factors that could affect their employment. During the interview, the counselor discusses each applicant's school promotion record and course failures to identify those youth who need summer remedial instruction. Together, the counselor and applicant develop an employment plan and determine whether the youth needs additional academic assistance. The counselor then arranges a summer job placement.

Applicants are referred one at a time to an employer for their job interview. Employers choose those they want to hire, although most hire the first referrals. Youth are hired to work twenty-five to thirty hours per week (depending on the type of placement) for seven weeks. In 1986, 1,297 youth were placed with 82 private-sector employers and 115 public and private nonprofit agencies.

The Summer Youth Employment Program offers job placements with or without academic or vocational enrichment activities. All participants are scheduled for a job readiness class, called the Labor Market Orientation Program. The two types of job placements and this class are described below.

Work Experience with Enrichment. In 1986, 527 young people were placed by interest and aptitude in jobs that included vocational enrichment or were supplemented with remedial instruction. These youth worked twenty-five hours at the job and participated in five hours of paid academic or vocational enrichment each week. All job placements with enrichment activities were developed in advance by the OJP.

The New Bedford Chamber of Commerce, under contract with the OJP, solicited private-sector employers to offer summer job placements and job-related enrichment activities. Potential employers outlined the proposed jobs' responsibilities and the content of the enrichment activities. The OJP, using JTPA funding, subsidized the youth's work experience; the employers in turn paid the youth's salary for time spent in the enrichment activities. In all, 139 young people were placed in private-sector jobs with a wide range of enrichment activities.

Several employers used management training exercises for the enrichment activities or had the youth shadow other employees or otherwise become familiar with the various jobs in a company. In one electronics company, three young people were hired to work in data processing, personnel, and accounting. As enrichment, they spent three weeks writing reports on the company and its products, the company's organization, and the function and responsibilities of their departments. In the remaining four weeks, they focused on computer applications in their departments, becoming familiar with personal computers and software and learning to set up and run a program. In another example, a youth was employed as an assistant in a health-food shop. The employer provided instruction in nutrition, health regulations, advertising, and the basics of bookkeeping and pricing.

Nonprofit companies that could provide work experience with enrichment were solicited through a grant proposal process. Nonprofit agencies that wanted a subsidized youth employee formally proposed a job and related learning experience to the OJP. In 1986, nineteen such agencies were awarded contracts for subsidized summer youth positions; 237 young people were placed in nonprofit agencies, schools, and city agencies. Related learning activities were provided on the site.

One example was a program of five day-care centers, where thirty-three girls aged sixteen and older worked as aides. They had daily one-hour classes in classroom training and child growth and development; at the end of the summer, they received a certificate in day-care training. In another example, a local high school used the summer job placements and funded enrichment activities to extend a school year program year-round.

When formal enrichment activities could not be structured in the workplace, the employers, with the assistance of the OJP staff, created homework assignments keyed to employment-related competencies. This was arranged for 127 participants.

Not all enrichment was vocation-related. Seventy-three youth were initially identified by the placement counselors as needing remediation and were willing to enroll in one of the three learning centers over the summer. The centers, run by the OJP, offered self-paced computerized instruction (using the Comprehensive Competencies Program developed by Remediation and Training Institute [RTI] in Washington, D.C.) for basic-skills remediation, GED preparation, and occupational exploration. Referred students were first tested for prescribed remedial instruction, usually in reading or math. Each week, in addition to twenty-five hours on the job, these youth worked five to ten hours on a selected subject, periodically testing their gains.

Work Experience Only. Applicants who are not interested in having a summer job with related instruction or academic assistance are placed in jobs providing work experience only. They work thirty hours per week, primarily in clerical positions and as laborers and aides with public or private non-profit agencies, earning the minimum wage ($3.55 per hour). In 1986, these summer positions ranged from clearing nature trails (twelve youth) to cataloguing and sweeping up in a glass museum (four youth). Eight young people worked with a local police department, primarily doing maintenance work. Another four were placed as peer counselors to work with children in a local migrant education program.

Special job placements are arranged for approximately 100 handicapped teenagers, all of whom are monitored by one job-placement counselor. Wherever possible, handicapped youth are placed in mainstream jobs; for example, a wheelchair-bound girl worked as a receptionist in a state agency. In other cases, specifically designed jobs are developed, often in maintenance positions.

Job Readiness Preparation. All youth in the program are required to participate in the Labor Market Orientation Program. Youth placed in jobs with enrichment classes attend one of seven Saturday classes prior to their job placement. These five-hour classes cover self-evaluation exercises and job-seeking and job-keeping skills.

Youth in jobs without enrichment have a shorter Labor Market Orientation Program delivered at their work site. A mobile van used as the classroom visits the various work sites throughout the summer, reaching about 90 percent of the youth. Six to eight young people per session spend two hours in job readiness instruction, learning about work habits and attitudes and how to prepare a résumé. They take an occupational interest test and review a videotape on occupations that interest them.

Employment preparation is not limited to these classes. The program staff strongly encourage the employers to reinforce good work habits among their summer employees. A heavy emphasis is placed on attendance. The program staff follow up with the employers if youth have poor attendance or work habits. If a youth is admonished about these problems more than once, the career specialists try to place him or her in another job. Each is given two or three chances before being dropped from the program.

Participants

The 1,297 young people who were placed in summer jobs in 1986 included roughly equal numbers of young men and women. Sixty-three percent were fourteen or fifteen years of age, 27 percent were sixteen or seventeen, and 10 percent were between eighteen and twenty-one. Thirty-nine percent of the youth were black or Hispanic. About 5 percent were school dropouts, 3 percent were high school graduates, and the rest were still in school. Seventy-nine percent of the youth had never worked before.

The program staff begins enrolling youth in the program at the end of March and accepts applicants until early July. All youth who are JTPA-eligible can be placed in the program. To be accepted, they must be between fourteen and twenty-one years of age, show proof of address and family income, and have a Social Security number. About 80 percent of those who apply are found to be eligible.

Most youth enrolled in the program are motivated and interested. About 5 percent turn out to be troublesome, requiring extra follow-up and transfers to other jobs. The program staff try to counsel the student and to provide follow-up services if family or abuse problems are found to exist.

In all, 527 youth were placed in summer jobs with enrichment and 770 in jobs without enrichment in 1986. Fifty-nine percent earned the minimum wage of $3.55 per hour, 30 percent earned $3.70 per hour, and 11 percent, primarily those in private-sector placements, earned $3.90 per hour. Ninety-two percent completed the seven weeks of summer employment. Sixty percent of the sixty-five school dropouts placed in the jobs program were subsequently enrolled in JTPA-funded employment and training programs.

Staffing and Administration

The program is overseen by two codirectors, who manage the day-to-day operations. Six career development and placement specialists match youth with the various jobs and oversee their activity throughout the summer. They are assisted by five field representatives, who visit each workplace at least weekly. Twice a day they report to their respective career specialists on how the jobs are going and discuss any problems that may have arisen. The field representatives may do on-site intervention as well, talking with the youth about their work responsibilities and working out difficulties between the youth and employers. If a problem exists, the career specialists may visit the workplace or call the young person in for counseling.

The program staff also includes fifty-one site counselors and field representatives and five intake and secretarial staff. Two instructors provide the Labor Market Orientation Program with the mobile van, one teaches the day-care center courses, and three operate the three learning centers with the assistance of three aides. The OJP also has three in-house monitors who visit each site to interview youth and employers. Their function is to be certain that the program's goals and objectives are being met. Any deficiencies they uncover are to be corrected within forty-eight hours.

Before starting the program, the OJP subcontracted with the New Bedford Chamber of Commerce to develop vocational exploration opportunities in the private sector. The chamber of commerce generated far more jobs than the OJP was able to fill. (The private-sector job placements had to be in a non-profit-making arm of a business, or it had to be demonstrated that the youth, whose salary was paid by JTPA funds, was not contributing to the profits of the company.) In addition, the OJP made grants to nineteen nonprofit agencies to provide work experience and related enrichment for JTPA-eligible youth, using JTPA funds to pay their salaries. The remaining jobs were developed by the OJP's counselors, arranged through past contacts and through employers participating in other OJP programs.

Funding

The program is funded through Title II-B of JTPA; it cost approximately $1.6 million in 1986. The funding pays the salaries of all employed youth and of the staff who administer the program. An additional $18,700 in private-sector employers' contributions was generated to pay for employed youths' enrichment activities, which total thirty-five hours per participant for the summer. To simplify the payment process, the OJP pays the young people their combined salary for work experience and enrichment and bills all employers at the end of the summer for the enrichment activities. Youth are paid only for the work and enrichment activities they attend.

Evaluation

The OJP has yet to perform a formal evaluation of the benefits of tying enrichment activities to summer job placements. They have received very good feedback on the youth from the employers who hired them, but they have no summary evidence on the academic or vocational gains or the post-program fate of these young people.

The staff, however, are striving to tie the enrichment activities to all of the program's summer jobs. They are planning to change from one-on-one to group counseling to provide more counseling and career planning time. They are also developing guidelines for other employment and training agencies on developing private-sector vocational exploration programs.

This program is a unique way of expanding the learning opportunities for youth in summer jobs. Moreover, the program staff attempt to look for young people with serious academic problems and steer them into a skills remediation program along with their job placement. This direct academic assistance for some participants, and the wider career exposure for almost half of those placed, should encourage these youth—statistically the group most likely to drop out—to remain in school. Only a follow-up evaluation can demonstrate how effectively the program is meeting this goal.

Summer Youth Employment Program

Program Components

- Short-term work experience program
- Summer job placements
- Work enrichment activities
- Basic-skills training

Program Inputs and Outcomes

- Target Population: JTPA-eligible youth (aged fourteen to twenty-one)
- Costs: $1,234 per youth for salary and placement; employer-contributed work experience; youth's salary enrichment
- Outcomes: Not ascertained

4

Removing Barriers to Staying in School: Helping Students Balance Family, Economic, and Educational Responsibilities

A significant percentage of youth dropouts report in later years that they left school for economic and family reasons. Schools that can help students juggle these responsibilities can encourage more students to complete high school. The three program summaries in this section show how schools removed certain barriers to schooling by offering specific solutions for students with special needs. These programs illustrate three different approaches to restructuring schools.

The first program is the Secondary Credit Exchange Program for migrant youth, which operates in nine Washington State school districts. Through evening classes, migrant students aged fourteen and older are given a chance to finish a school program they began in another state. Without the close communication and administrative coordination of programs between Washington schools and those in other states—primarily Texas and California—and the provision of evening instruction as an alternative to the regular high school, most of these migrant students could not graduate.

The second program is the Murray-Wright High School Day-Care Center in Detroit, Michigan. A day-care center at the school allows twenty Aid to Families with Dependent Children-

59

eligible (AFDC) teenage mothers to attend high school while their children are cared for in a well-structured environment. Without this free and accessible child care, many of these mothers would have had to quit school. The center is financed by state-administered federal social service funds.

The third program actually comprises two projects that originated in a school-based health clinic in a poor area of Houston, Texas. While delivering health care, family planning, and minor medical services to junior and senior high school students, the clinic administrators recognized a need for two dropout prevention programs. One is a case-management, social service program for thirty high-risk preadolescent boys. The other is an employment training and basic-skills remediation program for teenage mothers. The latter is supplemented by on-site daycare services for their infants and the clinic's medical and social services. The health clinic serves as a focal point for identifying barriers to continued education and supplements the new programs.

These three programs illustrate ways in which programs can be designed to address the special needs of students and allow them to continue their regular school program; they also show how to tap state and federal resources specifically designed for those needs. These resources include subsidized daycare, employment and training, health care, and compensatory education services.

SECONDARY CREDIT EXCHANGE PROGRAM
Washington State

Without a way of continuing their education program in different school districts and states, few migrant students would ever be able to complete high school. Migrant children often attend regular school during the winter months when little work is available. But when their families migrate north in the spring, perhaps coming from Texas and California to cut asparagus and pick strawberries, their schooling is disrupted. While younger children continue going to school in Washington, during the summer and early fall, older children usually work in the fields along with their parents, picking berries and apples. The Secondary Credit Exchange Program enables older students to continue school by means of evening and summer school instruction.

Through intricate coordination between nine Washington school districts and the migrant students' home school districts —at least thirty in Texas, California, and elsewhere in Washington—Washington State provides instruction for between 650 and 750 migrant youth. Each student's program is matched to a home-based course of study to provide the instructional hours necessary to complete the school year. For six to ten weeks, migrant students in grades 7 through 12 receive four or five hours of individual and class instruction, and often a meal, after work. A summer school program is offered in two districts, giving students another opportunity to catch up and to complete credit hours. At the end of the spring term and summer program, successfully completed credit hours are transferred back to the students' home school districts for course credit. While no summary program information is available, state officials report that most students are able to complete in Washington four courses begun in Texas.

The program is supported by local basic education funds, supplemented with federal compensatory education funds targeted for migrant students. Without it, few youth migrating annually to Washington State would finish a school year or progress through high school on schedule without sacrificing their wages. This program shows how local school districts can adjust their structure to the employment needs of those they are to educate. Equally important, it is an example of how states and their districts can work cooperatively in managing a joint education program.

Background

The transient life style and the family's need for their wages keep adolescents out of school. In 1980, 422,000 children nationwide, including 84,000 adolescents, followed the seasonal crops from state to state with their families. There are no estimates available, however, on the number of youth who migrate north to Washington State every March when their families, mostly from southern and southwestern Texas, come to cut asparagus in the rural Yakima valley and Columbia Basin and to pick strawberries and other crops in the Skagit area. While the younger children continue going to day schools, those thirteen and older typically stay out of school, getting up at 3:30 A.M. to pick crops until early afternoon. Often, these older children attended regular day school in Texas or California but left before completing any courses.

The first Secondary Credit Exchange Program was developed in 1970 by a second-grade teacher to serve the older siblings of her students who were not coming to school because they were needed in the fields. The teacher offered to tutor the students on her own time if her principal could arrange with the students' home schools to grant credit for work completed. He contacted each school; all agreed. That spring, the teacher tutored six students in the evenings at the local labor camp. Their excellent progress was recorded and transmitted to their home schools. Thus the credit exchange program began.

The next year, the program was supported by federal compensatory education funds targeting migrant children and continued to serve migrant students in the district. By 1974, thirty-five students from ten schools in Texas and California were being taught. In 1975, four Washington and four Texas districts with high numbers of migrant youth were added to the program. A formal credit transfer agreement was developed for these districts; all other districts continued to participate without a formal agreement. The Washington State Supervisor of Migrant Education approved funding and expansion of this formal arrangement; an advisory committee of eight superintendents was formed and a project coordinator was appointed. Through this arrangement, the Texas school districts were responsible for getting lists of students, course requirements, class schedules, and other information to the Washington school districts. In turn, Washington was to provide formal instruction and record completed course credits, which were to be transmitted on official school transcripts.

In 1977, the state applied for and received Joint Dissemination Review Panel approval to qualify as a National Diffusion Network–approved project, thereby receiving funds for program dissemination. By this time, eighteen Washington districts and fifty Texas districts were coordinating instruction for 550 students. The program was expanded in 1982 to include summer school. In 1986, the program was reduced to just nine school districts for the spring term and two other districts for the summer program, reflecting changes in the availability of seasonal work.

In 1981, a regional conference served as a forum in which to formalize program policy issues between Texas and Washington school districts and to begin setting up exchange programs between Texas and other states. Since then, ten or twelve other states have set up similar spring or summer programs.

Previously, state staff annually visited the students' home school districts to collect information on course requirements and schedules. In 1986, the state began to rely on the Migrant Student Record Transfer System (MSRTS), a national system that has recently been expanded to cover secondary course information, thereby easing the transmission of information from district to district.

Description

The Secondary Credit Exchange Program is essentially an evening junior and senior high school program that provides as much educational continuity as possible for each migrant secondary student. Each home-base or sending school district defines the curriculum and course of study recommended for each student; the receiving schools try to match and complete them.

Since the programs operate primarily in the spring (but can occasionally be arranged during the regular school year), staff in receiving Washington State districts begin in the winter to plan their programs and apply to the state education agency for supplemental funding. In early March, the sending school districts record and transmit pertinent student information on the automated data system (the MSRTS) to be used in planning migrating students' programs in Washington.

The sending school district counselors recruit migrant students for the program before they move north with their families. Later, when migrant families arrive in Washington State, a home liaison worker from each participating Washington district visits the local labor camps to explain the program to children and parents and to encourage the field supervisors to send all eligible youth to school at the end of the work day. Posters are put up around the labor camp, in stores, laundromats, and churches, describing the program and encouraging students to attend.

The evening school programs are usually housed in local district high schools or other centrally located facilities. Transportation and meals are often provided; extracurricular activities are rarely offered.

In 1986, nine school districts provided evening school for 650 to 750 students in grades 7 through 12. Programs ranged in size from 7 to 254 students; classes served from 12 to 25 students per teacher, with teachers' aides assisting in larger classes. Students are scheduled by grade and study four or five academic subjects during the evening. The evening school program usually runs for six to ten weeks, Monday through Thursday, 4 to 8 P.M., depending on each district's design.

Instruction focuses on basic education skills, using teacher-made materials or materials purchased especially for the program. Local textbooks are used if they follow the same instructional sequence as the students' home-school courses require. In some cases, the sending schools forward textbooks and instructional materials. More typically, the program teachers prepare worksheets and activities for instruction.

Students can sign up for self-paced course work in up to two classes, making use of the Washington State Portable Assisted Study Sequence (PASS) program, a self-paced instructional course developed in California. A PASS unit covers eighteen hours of work per subject and is available for a number of courses. Schools typically schedule students for these module lessons if they need the courses to graduate or are already scheduled for four classes, are still deficient in credits, and can handle the additional work independently.

While each district organizes its own program, a summary of how two districts structure theirs illustrates typical Secondary Credit Exchange Programs.

The tiny town of Mabton, with a population of 1,250, swells every spring as migrant families move into the fourteen labor camps located within the school district's boundaries. In 1986, Mabton's evening school enrolled 180 students from over twenty-three districts, mostly in Texas. A six-week program in basic skills is offered for grades 7 through 12, covering biology, general science, math, social studies, and language arts. All classes are grouped by subject, and students rotate among teachers through five periods. The school is staffed by ten teachers, seven aides, a part-time home visitor, and a part-time director.

In 1986, 180 students were registered by the second day of school; about 20 students were signed up for PASS courses, which provided some of the course work they needed to graduate. Mabton uses its own textbooks. To use all available time for classes, it is assumed that students will eat at home, and meals are not provided.

Pasco, a larger town at the confluence of the Snake and Columbia rivers, has the largest secondary credit night school program in the state. About 250 students are enrolled in grades 8 through 12, most in grades 8 and 9. All but 4 percent of the students are Hispanic, primarily Mexican American. Ninety-five percent of the students return each year, except for the seniors, who often remain in their home-base school to graduate. Most of the twenty-six twelfth graders enrolled in 1986 will graduate in Pasco.

The program is divided into four periods between 5 and 8:20 P.M. Fourteen teachers, aided by paraprofessionals, cover basic curriculum areas. Students are scheduled only for required courses or needed credit areas on their sending school schedule. They can take up to two more courses through the PASS program. Students are scheduled for physical education if they are deficient in this subject. Although all students are eligible, only half come early for the free dinner in the cafeteria.

The staff members are selected from the district's regular day teachers, substitute teachers, and others. All are state-certified; some teachers and all the paraprofessionals are bilingual. Additional project staff include the director, the secretary, six bus drivers, and the kitchen workers. The director recently created an advisory council of six elected seniors who represent the students at school board meetings and provide feedback on special activities. Attendance and discipline are strictly enforced; absenteeism is reviewed daily by the program director and the home liaison, who follow up with parents and employers.

Participants

No summary statistical information is available on the characteristics of the 650 to 750 migrant students who enrolled in the 1986 Secondary Credit Exchange Program or on their academic achievements in the program. School officials report that most students are Mexican American and for many, English is a second language. While boys and girls are equally likely to enroll, girls are more likely to graduate.

The program is structured for students who have migrated to Washington State and must work in the fields during the day. Program directors try to discourage formerly migratory children whose families have settled in the community for a year or more from leaving school in the spring to pick crops. Staff in the receiving districts recruit students through the sending schools and later from the labor camps.

The school districts work cooperatively with the employers and crew leaders to encourage school-age workers to come to the evening program. The schools have some leverage here, since fourteen- and fifteen-year-olds cannot work if they do not attend the evening program.

Overall, this is a difficult population to recruit; not all who migrate with their families enroll in the evening program. School staff speculate that the hard work during the day and extra family chores and responsibilities prevent some students from coming to school in the evening. Sometimes parents will not let their children come or the children are not interested. In some cases, too, youth are in communities where a program is not available. Yet no information exists on the number of eligible students who enroll or who drop out of school. Nonetheless, the school districts and the employers make a good effort to encourage students to come to school and keep up academically.

The local school districts run the evening programs with the same attendance, discipline, and course-completion policies as the day school programs. Students who are absent or truant excessively or who are discipline problems can be suspended or dropped from the program, but this rarely occurs. Whether it is a close relationship between district staff and the camp supervisor, the discipline and attendance practices of the sending school districts, the social benefits of the evening school, or the students' own strong motivation to complete school, attendance and discipline are usually not problems in the program.

Staffing and Administration

The program is under the direction of the Washington State Migrant Education staff in the Division of Instruction and Supplemental Programs, Office of the Superintendent of Public Instruction. In addition to the central staff, two regional centers provide technical assistance. An eastern Washington school district operates the state's MSRTS.

Each school district's Secondary Credit Exchange Program is managed by a director and staffed by teachers (one per fifteen or twenty students), paraprofessionals (one per one or two teachers), a home visitor, and support staff, such as secretaries, bus drivers, and cafeteria staff, as needed. All teachers are state-certified, and an effort is made to recruit bilingual teachers and paraprofessionals.

A very cooperative relationship exists between the Washington and Texas local school districts and state staff in sharing information on the students and transferring credits. Between 100 and 125 Texas school districts are now participating in the credit accrual process with districts in ten to twelve states. The longest relationship, of course, is with Washington, where the official Secondary Credit Exchange Program began. The Texas school districts' guidance counselors for migrant youth are assisted by the state's Migrant Interstate Program in coordinating their students' course needs through the exchange process. Yet despite the problems of tracking students, it is rare that records of course hours earned in Washington are not accepted by Texas school districts and applied toward a student's course credit.

While communication is good between the two states, it can break down in the transmission of quantities of information among school districts and in scheduling students in a very short time. The sending and receiving schools cannot always predict where students are migrating. The sending schools are not always timely in forwarding student information, and frequently the receiving schools must guess at the sequence of instruction a student's scheduled courses are to cover. Added to this is the lack of curricular materials and course books; the Washington school districts try to adapt their materials as well as possible. Texas and Washington school district and state officials meet regularly to reduce these problems. In addition, Washington staff attend Texas's annual conference, where they jointly review program problems and share new ideas.

Every spring, the Washington State education agency holds meetings for migrant education staff across the state to discuss resource issues and problems, such as the use of the MSRTS and credit transferring. State officials cannot require that such programs as the Secondary Credit Exchange be provided, since school districts are autonomous. But state officials can promote the program to local districts through various state conferences and meetings. In the summer, for example, the Office of the Superintendent of Public Instruction sponsors a statewide conference at which several sessions usually discuss the Secondary Credit Exchange Program.

Funding

Washington State receives a federal migrant education allocation to provide several educational programs, including the Secondary Credit Exchange Program. In turn, the state education department subcontracts with seventy-five school districts for migrant education programs. These federal compensatory education funds for migrant student services are to supplement basic state education programs and funds provided for each student in attendance. Nine districts provide a spring term evening school and two other districts provide evening summer school for secondary students. The cost and allocation of funding for the evening program cannot be estimated.

Evaluation

The Secondary Credit Exchange Program has not been evaluated since its early days. In 1977, the program staff provided evidence of program effectiveness to gain National Diffusion Network–approved status. According to the report, few migrant youth working in the harvest enrolled in secondary school at the work site before the program. The program has been exceedingly popular since its initiation, growing from 35 students in 1974 to 550 students in 1977. Only 2.5 percent of those enrolled dropped out of the program in 1976. The report did not demonstrate, however, the long-term educational gains of the students.

The main problem in running the program is not being able to establish a course of study for the enrolled students in a short time. One reason is the difficulty of obtaining students' program information promptly. Even now, the school districts' use of the MSRTS to share student information is not always efficient or comprehensive. Often there is insufficient information to plan courses and schedule students. Use of the system is improving. Washington officials reported that in 1986, Texas made placement information through the MSRTS for over 80 percent of the students enrolling in Washington.

The second reason is that the receiving school districts can never be certain how many and what ages of students will enroll each spring. As the program staff describe it, the dynamics of migration make it very difficult to anticipate program needs. Changes in the crops and the weather affect the patterns of migration and thus the number of students enrolling in the program. Regardless of all these problems, all districts try to have their programs under way by the second day. Finally, because of time constraints, the program can generally provide instruction only in four or fewer of the six courses students were probably taking at their sending schools.

The Washington State and Texas school districts have instituted a simple, although administratively complex, program to offer migrant secondary students an opportunity for continuous education. Despite the lack of information on its effectiveness, the program is obviously necessary and well used.

Secondary Credit Exchange Program

Program Components

- Accessible comprehensive instructional program for working students
- Interstate student record transfer system
- Cooperative relationship among school districts
- Evening school program
- Focus on basic skills

Program Inputs and Outcomes

- Target population: Secondary school migrant youth
- Costs: Unknown
- Outcomes: Unknown

MURRAY-WRIGHT HIGH SCHOOL DAY-CARE CENTER
Detroit, Michigan

Recognizing that poor teenage mothers would be unable to complete their high school education without day-care assistance, staff from Murray-Wright High School established an on-site center for infants and toddlers in 1974. Eligible teenage mothers can drop off their children (aged six weeks to two-and-a-half years) at the center before school begins and attend their high school classes, assured that their children are receiving appropriate care. First-year mothers are required to participate in a year-long parenting class, learning about maternal and child health care, child rearing, and problem solving. A teacher-coordinator and day-care center staff provide a structured and supportive environment for teenage mothers and their children throughout the school year. They encourage the mothers to complete their education, to avoid a second pregnancy while still in school, and to follow proper child-care practices.

Since its beginning, the center has helped twenty adolescent mothers each year stay in school. Up to 75 percent have been able to graduate from high school, and a few have subsequently pursued postsecondary education. The program administrators have been able to defray the costs of the day-care center by funding it in part through state-administered federal social services funds. This program illustrates an effective way for two public service systems—education and social services—to direct assistance to poor teenage mothers, giving them a chance to complete their schooling.

Background

The Detroit public school system serves 190,000 students from kindergarten through twelfth grade, including 51,500 students in twenty-four high schools. Almost 14 percent of the high school students drop out each year, only 55 percent of entering ninth graders are likely to graduate. Parenthood is a common reason for girls to drop out of school. Like other depressed urban areas, Detroit has an extremely high teenage birthrate—4,300 adolescent girls gave birth in 1980, yielding a rate of 83 per 1,000.

Currently, the Detroit public schools operate three alternative programs for pregnant and parenting teenage girls. In addition to providing academic instruction for the 236 girls served annually, the programs offer prenatal and parenting instruction. While these programs provide needed personal support to young mothers none offer day-care facilities for the infants so that the mothers can continue school.

One school does provide such a service, however. In 1974, a home economics department supervisor proposed establishing a school-based day-care center at Murray-Wright High School in response to a request from students. Murray-Wright already had a preschool day-care center, established in 1971 as a laboratory for the school's child-care training program. The laboratory center is a licensed day-care center for twenty-five preschoolers aged two-and-a-half to five years; the related training program was supported through federal vocational education funds.

The home economics supervisor, with support from her principal, worked with staff from the Michigan Department of Social Services (DSS) to design a program that would meet their funding requirements. The creation of a teenage mothers' day-care center met with some opposition from a few members of the Detroit public schools central office staff who thought the services would encourage teenage parenthood. But the school was able to overcome this with strong support from the local community and the central board of education, coupled with the availability of state funding. The program was established in 1974; from the beginning it was inundated with requests from students wanting to enroll their children.

The program has enjoyed a stable existence with low staff turnover since its inception. A nurse has worked in the program since it began, and only two teacher-coordinators have directed the program. Despite administrative turnover within the high school and the school system, the day-care program has maintained strong school and district support.

The day-care center is one of many dropout prevention programs in the high school. Two community-based organizations conduct group counseling programs to encourage high-risk students to stay in school, working with about eighty students altogether. Another thirty ninth and tenth graders are enrolled in Upward Bound, through which they attend local colleges after school and on weekends to receive assistance in improving their basic academic skills. Finally, one school counselor has been assigned to work with 150 ninth-grade students who have attendance and academic problems. As a result of these programs and a few vocational training programs, the 2,400 students at Murray-Wright High School have a cumulative graduation rate of 63 percent, 15 percent higher than the citywide average.

Description

The infant-toddler day-care center, with its adjacent parenting education classroom, is housed near a laboratory preschool day-care center (for two-and-a-half- to five-year-old children) and an adjacent child development training classroom in Murray-Wright High School. The teenage mothers who have children enrolled in the infant-toddler center attend regular high school classes and, if they are first-year mothers, take a yearlong parenting education class. The program's design reflects the philosophy that teenage mothers should not be treated differently from other high school students and that every effort should be made to integrate them fully into the regular high school program. Yet there is an understanding that the young mothers need assistance with their new parental role, so that program staff are available in the center or in the parenting education classroom for informal counseling and social service referrals.

Teenage Mothers' Program. The mothers' school day begins just before 8 A.M., when they drop their children off before starting school. Some of the twenty mothers come early enough to help prepare the children's breakfast, but most barely have time to leave their children and run to class.

All first-year mothers are scheduled for a parenting education course during the school's third period. This year-long course, taught by the center's teacher-coordinator, covers child rearing from birth and problem-solving techniques. The class enrolls up to twenty students and is open to all high school students; teenage mothers are given first priority and make up 75 percent of the class. The classwork is structured around a textbook, *The Caring Parent;* special emphasis is given to discussing the problems of child abuse, substance abuse, sexually transmitted diseases, contraception, and sexuality in general.

As part of this class and as an extracurricular activity for the mothers, the teacher-coordinator sponsors a parenting club. Usually, the girls organize fund-raising events, such as a fashion show, and put the money toward club activities and materials for the day-care center. The club is affiliated with Future Homemakers of America; with the money they raise, the girls can afford to attend the association's state conference.

The teenage mothers are enrolled in a full academic program in the high school. They are not grouped for any class or homeroom except the required parenting course for first-year mothers. Only a few mothers enroll in one of the several vocational training programs available in the high school. Their pregnancies and early parenthood often limit the time they have to complete all the high school courses required for graduation. Enrolling in a vocational training program would often require them to remain in school longer; few teenage mothers therefore opt for these programs, including the child development training program. The day-care center's hours also limit the number of school activities the teenage mothers can participate in, unless alternate child care can be arranged.

Most support services for the teenage mothers are provided informally by the teacher-coordinator and the center staff. The teacher-coordinator becomes a close adviser for the mothers throughout their time in high school. She acts as a case manager, referring the mothers as needed to appropriate social service agencies, such as public assistance and housing. Through the years, she has developed a close working relationship with local social service agencies. At times she helps transport students to and from school, recognizing the difficulty young mothers have in getting themselves and their children ready for school, especially on cold winter days. Public school transportation is available, but it is limited to students living more than a mile and a half from the school, a long distance for a girl to walk with a young infant.

The coordinator and center staff also try informally to encourage the girls to postpone future childbearing until after they complete high school. This is a sensitive position for the staff to take, because at the same time, they make a tremendous effort not to stigmatize the girls for having had a child. They encourage the students to plan for their own future and economic independence.

School-Based Day-Care Center. The infant-toddler center, established for the children of teenage mothers enrolled in the high school, cares for twenty children aged six weeks to two-and-a-half years. It opens just before school begins and closes just after the final period. The children are cared for by a full-time nurse, two paraprofessionals, the teacher-coordinator, and various student volunteers.

The center's schedule is divided into the same periods as the high school's schedule. All children are fed during the first period with food provided by the cafeteria and supplemented by the center's program for a balanced diet. Afterward, the children are cleaned up and have free play until the second period. On Mondays, Wednesdays, and Fridays, the paraprofessional and volunteer students conduct lessons on basic concepts during the second period; on Tuesdays and Thursdays, the toddlers are taken into the adjoining classroom for a music lesson. Third period is lunch, again provided by the school cafeteria. Afterward, the children are put down for a nap, often with the volunteer students reading stories. As the children wake up during fifth period, they have free play until snack time at sixth period. If it is nice outside, the staff and students will take the children out during seventh period for a walk or other activity before getting them ready to go home.

The day-care center staff make every effort to involve the mothers in planning and caring for their children as well as to guide them informally in proper child-rearing methods. When the teenage mothers enroll their children in the program, they fill out forms about the care their children need, including feeding or discipline requirements. The center staff tries to follow these instructions in order to reinforce the way each mother is raising her child. The center staff talk informally about child rearing with each mother when she drops off or picks up her child or drops by the center during the day. It gives the mothers a chance to ask questions or learn different ways of interacting with their children, and it gives the staff a chance to dispel any misconceptions the young mothers might have about child rearing.

Participants

Adolescent mothers learn about the day-care center program through their counselors, teachers, and friends. The infant-toddler center does no special outreach to recruit teenage mothers. The girls apply for acceptance in the program and are interviewed by the teacher-coordinator to determine their eligibility. Only AFDC-eligible mothers who are two years below grade level in reading and math can qualify. Applying students must complete their AFDC-qualification paperwork before enrolling. While the program is only for mothers attending Murray-Wright High School, girls can transfer to Murray-Wright in order to participate.

Since the program has so few places for children and their mothers, the coordinator selects only those girls who are committed to completing school and are likely to do so. For example, experience has shown that teenage mothers with more than one child are unable to juggle school and child rearing and will drop out; such mothers are not accepted into the program. In addition, mothers whose children have serious medical problems are not accepted, since the day-care center is not equipped to handle them. While the program does have clear eligibility guidelines, exceptions are made at the staff's discretion.

More girls request placement in the program than can be accommodated. The teacher-coordinator keeps a waiting list and enrolls eligible students on a first-come, first-served basis. Few other options exist for teenage mothers. If places open up when enrolled mothers complete school, move, or drop out, new students can be enrolled in the program, but only up to the sixth week of each semester; after that they must wait until the next semester.

The DSS, through its funding of the program, restricts center eligibility to children of teenage mothers receiving AFDC. In 1980, the DSS tightened the eligibility requirements for subsidized day-care services, making it more difficult for some girls to qualify for the program. Now, if an AFDC-eligible teenage mother has someone at home who can take care of her child, she is not eligible to enroll her child in the school's day-care center.

The center's staff has observed that the adolescent mothers usually have a number of serious personal problems that further increase the difficulty of being a high school student and a mother simultaneously. The staff estimates that 25 to 50 percent of the teenage mothers drop out of the program and school, usually because of the stress they face. Repeat pregnancies are rare among the mothers who stay in the program, however, reflecting the desire of the girls to finish school and the success of the program staff in encouraging them to postpone further childbearing. The staff estimated that in the last five years, only two girls have had a second child while in school.

Teenage mothers are dropped from the program only if they are not attending school. If they are having academic difficulty, the program staff will try to arrange tutoring assistance. The staff members make a concerted effort to encourage good school attendance and ultimate completion.

While the program staff keep individual student records, they do not record how well each group of mothers does in school and beyond. Therefore, no information exists on the number of mothers who completed high school and, of those, the number who went on to postsecondary training or a job.

Staffing and Administration

The Murray-Wright Day-Care Center is part of the Home Economics/Vocational Education Division of the high school. One teacher coordinates the infant-toddler center and the parenting education course for the teenage mothers. The center is also staffed by a nurse and two paraprofessionals. (The DSS requires a ratio of one staff member to every four to six children, depending on the children's ages.) Since Detroit high school students must do 200 hours of approved work and community service as part of the graduation requirements, the center also has some student volunteers. About two students volunteer each period to help in the center.

The day-care center is licensed through the DSS, which establishes operating guidelines. Every two years, DSS inspectors visit the site and conduct a review, preceded by health department and fire department inspections.

Funding

The program is supported by a mixture of local school district funds, Chapter 1 (federal compensatory education) monies, and social services funds. The total annual budget for the infant-toddler center and the parenting education class, excluding space and utilities, is roughly $82,000, or $4,100 per mother and child when twenty mothers are enrolled. This covers the staff salaries, food, and resource materials.

The DSS reimburses the center for each eligible child in attendance. In 1985-86, the reimbursement rates were $11.04 per day per infant, yielding $13,000 for the year. These funds cover the cost of some insurance, food, toys, diapers and other supplies, and part of the staff salaries. Local Detroit public school funds cover the teacher-coordinator and paraprofessional salaries. The remaining salary costs are covered by federal compensatory education funds. The school district also provides space, utilities, and some insurance costs.

State social services reimbursements total only 40 percent of the center's potential income from this source (20 placements at $11.04 per day for 180 days would yield $40,000). The reason the clinic receives so much less than its potential DSS income, according to district budget staff, is that reimbursements are made only for days when eligible infants are in attendance. High mother and infant absenteeism, student turnover, and placement of noneligible children in the program reduces the center's actual income from DSS reimbursements. An even greater problem, however, is the loss of income while a mother's eligibility is being determined, a process that can take up to six weeks.

Evaluation

The program has never been evaluated; while records are kept on enrolled teenage mothers while they are in the program, they are not maintained after the mothers have graduated. Although a needs assessment has never been done, the staff senses that the center is far too limited for the needs of high school students. They estimate that at least forty-five girls at Murray-Wright High School alone would qualify for the center if space were available for their children.

To determine how effective the program is in helping teenage mothers complete their high school education, more information is needed on those in the program, and a comparison must be made with similar teenage mothers who are not enrolled in the program. Despite the lack of information, we believe the program strategy is a valid means of helping teenage mothers stay in school. Educators and policy makers have similarly recognized the need to provide day-care assistance for teenage mothers. To this end, the federal Women's Educational Equity Act Program has funded the New York City–based Academy for Educational Development to prepare a manual on setting up school-based day-care centers for teenage mothers.

The Murray-Wright program also illustrates an effective way for two public service agencies to combine services and resources for one target population. By strategically placing the day-care center in the high school, the social service agency helps the school encourage teenage mothers to complete their high school education.

Murray-Wright High School Day-Care Center

Program Components

- School-based infant-toddler day-care center
- Year-long parenting education program
- Integration with regular high school program

Program Inputs and Outcomes

- Target population: Low-achieving AFDC-eligible teenage mothers
- Costs: DSS daily reimbursements of $11.04 per child in the center; contributed space and utilities; Chapter 1–funded support staff
- Outcomes: 50–75 percent of teenage mothers graduate

ADOLESCENT PRIMARY HEALTH CARE CLINIC
Houston, Texas

The Adolescent Primary Health Care Clinic, closely affiliated with eight junior and senior high schools in a poor area of Houston, has initiated dropout prevention and dropout service programs that draw on the clinic's medical and counseling resources.

The clinic, operated by the Urban Affairs Corporation, expanded its initial interest in delivering health services to deal directly with the dropout problem through a multiservice approach. A group of thirty dropout-prone preadolescent boys in one junior high school are engaged in an intensive counseling and tutoring program in an attempt to instill in them an interest in education and to assist them in coping with personal problems. Another program provides job training, remedial education, and other support services to 150 pregnant and parenting adolescent girls, helping them to complete their education and attain economic independence. Both programs draw on the medical care, social services, and counseling and referral resources of the clinic.

In some ways, the clinic itself can be viewed as a dropout prevention program, because it screens students for serious health problems that may be barriers to school completion. The clinic offers a range of health care services, including medical screenings, acute medical care, prenatal and postpartum care, pediatric screening, family planning, and social and psychological services.

The dropout prevention and service programs are funded separately by a mixture of foundation and Texas Department of Human Services funds. Space and resources are contributed by the Houston Independent School District. The clinic's health services and its two dropout prevention programs operate year-round.

Background

Houston, like the rest of Texas, is plagued with a severe economic and employment crisis stemming from deeply depressed oil and farming industries. After a period of rapid population growth during the 1970s, the city's population has stabilized at 1.8 million. The current unemployment rate is over 10 percent and is considerably higher among youth (21 percent) and blacks (15 percent). The Houston public school enrollment, among the largest in the nation, is also predominantly minority. In 1984–85, the school population was 187,000, of which 44 percent were black, 34 percent Hispanic, 19 percent white, and the remainder Asian.

Both Texas and Houston have made strong program commitments to reducing the number of youth dropouts. The scope of Houston's dropout problem cannot yet be adequately calculated, although it is known to be large. The district's school records do not differentiate between students who drop out and those who transfer elsewhere. The district's most recent effort to address its dropout problem has been to draft a "Comprehensive Dropout Prevention and Reclamation Program" plan; the plan has not been funded because the system is facing a dramatic fiscal crisis and changes in administration.

The Urban Affairs Corporation (UAC) began in 1972 as a private, nonprofit human services agency in response to the lack of quality child care for low-income families. The UAC's health clinic in Houston's Fifth Ward is one of the few school-based mechanisms for screening and addressing some of the problems limiting students' ability to stay in school. The Fifth Ward is one of the poorest in the city and, by most indexes, one of the most deprived. The incidence of poverty, unemployment, adolescent pregnancy, female heads of households, and families on public assistance are all above the citywide averages. Ninety percent of its 65,400 residents are black (in contrast to 26 percent in Houston overall).

The impetus to establish a school-based health clinic appeared in 1979 when the UAC approached the Houston Independent School District for space for a day-care center. The discussions turned to the problems of teenage pregnancy, the need for child care for adolescent mothers, and the broader health care needs of these young girls. The school district agreed to provide space for a day-care center and to support the UAC's development of a health clinic. With substantial foundation funding, the UAC opened a clinic in June 1981, targeting the 8,000 students enrolled in seven schools clustered in the Fifth Ward. (An eighth school was added later.) The Houston Independent School District provided free space and utilities for the clinic and a UAC-run day-care center in a converted junior high school, into which the UAC subsequently moved its central administrative offices.

Following the establishment of the clinic, the UAC launched two new programs to address the needs of high-risk youth beyond the scope of clinical health care. The first was the Training and Employment for Adolescent Mothers (TEAM) project, which provides education, training, and employment to pregnant teenagers and young mothers. The second was the Fifth Ward Enrichment Program, which offers educational and enrichment activities for preadolescent boys considered to be potential dropouts.

The UAC's staff, along with the Texas State Department of Human Services (which funds the day-care center), were increasingly concerned about teenage mothers who often left school to have their babies, did not return, and were unemployable. The UAC designed a program to help these girls attain self-sufficiency through job training and employment. Initially, the TEAM program was to operate during the summer, as a bridge for the girls into permanent employment or reentry in school by September. After two summers, however, the program staff found that three months of after-school training and twelve weeks of on-the-job work experience were inadequate for these young mothers. They expanded the program to a full year and renamed it TEAM II. The new program began full-time, year-round operations in September 1985 with a large contract from the Texas Department of Human Services.

The Fifth Ward Enrichment Program was developed in the spring of 1984 from informal discussions between the clinic director and the project director of another Houston youth program serving high-risk adolescents. Both felt a need to design an early intervention program for preadolescent boys having a difficult transition from elementary to middle school. The ideas evolved quickly into a funded dropout prevention program, consisting of after-school tutoring and activities and intensive counseling and follow-up, for a group of boys identified as potential dropouts.

Description, Participants, and
Staffing and Administration

The two dropout prevention and service programs are independent, although closely affiliated with the adolescent health clinic. A summary description of the clinic and the two programs follows.

School-Based Health Clinic. The school-based Adolescent Primary Health Care Clinic currently makes health services available to 10,000 students enrolled in eight junior and senior high schools in Houston's Fifth Ward. It is located in one of the targeted schools, in an outbuilding connected by a walkway to the main school building. The clinic provides screening and primary and preventive health care to students living in the targeted area. Family planning and prenatal and postpartum care are priority services.

The clinic operates as a comprehensive adolescent health care center. It is open Monday through Friday from 8 A.M. to 6 P.M. year-round. It provides free health care to all eligible students and their children, including medical screenings and sports physicals, family planning, treatment of minor illnesses, and prenatal, postpartum, and pediatric care. The family planning services are supplemented by sex education seminars taught in the target schools and by individual and group counseling sessions. Social services, including outreach and advocacy, are available primarily for pregnant and parenting teenagers; a structured parenting education program is offered, and home visits are made. Individual and group psychological sessions are provided to clients referred by the medical staff. Limited transportation is available for students to and from school for their clinic visits.

Almost 1,100 students were served by the clinic in 1984–

85 (14 percent of the target population), each visiting twice, on the average. Of the students receiving medical care, 92 percent were black, in keeping with the racial makeup of the area. Sixty-nine percent were between fourteen and eighteen years of age, and 61 percent were female. About 50 percent were AFDC-certified and many of the rest were probably eligible.

Since most clinic clients have not had a complete physical since early childhood, the clinic's medical screenings provide a needed opportunity to identify serious medical problems. The most common clinic visits are for family planning, minor acute illnesses, obstetrical care, and athletic physicals. Less frequently, the clinic is used for pediatric visits.

The clinic staff includes a clinic manager, two social workers, a health educator, a pediatrician, a nurse practitioner, a vocational nurse, a clinic attendant, and a part-time driver. One pediatrician and one obstetrician-gynecologist each spend one day per week at the clinic, through the clinic's contract with the University of Texas Health Science Center at Houston. The physicians usually bring between two and five medical residents with them to assist in serving students.

Training and Employment for Adolescent Mothers (TEAM) II. Housed with the clinic is a training program serving over 200 pregnant and parenting teenage girls. The program offers a comprehensive case-management program, including day care for children aged two weeks through six years, medical services for both mothers and their children, preemployment and vocational training, on-the-job training and assistance in gaining permanent job placements, and educational services, primarily GED preparation and remedial instruction.

According to UAC materials, the program's goal is to "assist adolescent mothers in becoming productive, self-sufficient, contributing members of society, thereby eliminating social service dependency." Specific objectives mention obtaining health care, avoidance of future pregnancies, use of counseling and referral services, elimination of welfare dependency, and educational and occupational achievements. In carrying out these objectives, the program integrates existing UAC services with those of other local organizations and agencies through cooperative agreements. The program explicitly targets the dual problems of teenage pregnancy and dropping out of school. As a dropout service effort, it encourages teenage mothers to return to high school or community college to complete their education.

No formal recruitment is necessary; through word-of-mouth referrals, the demand exceeds the slots available. To enroll, all girls must be currently pregnant or a mother, fourteen to twenty-two years of age, and eligible for AFDC.

Upon entry into the program, participants are assigned to a program counselor who coordinates and follows up on their service needs. Each girl can use four program components as needed: education, preemployment, job training, and health care from the clinic. Fifty pregnant teens receive prenatal care, including high-risk intervention, while the 150 teen mothers receive postpartum care.

The program started with the assumption that most of the girls enrolled would still be in high school. The staff found that most participants had poor academic preparation and were unable to keep up with high school work. About 80 percent of the girls enrolled had already dropped out of school and lacked even basic reading skills. The program emphasis was thus shifted to on-site remedial instruction and pre-GED classes.

The mothers are offered preemployment classes, for which they are paid a stipend at the minimum wage rate. These classes are a prerequisite for placement in permanent employment through the program. Through the classes, the job counselors attempt to help each girl develop career plans and seek job placements for on-the-job training; counselors monitor the performance of the girls who are placed with regular follow-up support sessions. The program has public funding for 133 subsidized job placements.

The program's twelve staff members are a program director, an assistant director, a job developer, a social worker, three counselors (preemployment, on-the-job training, and pregnancy), a case-management director, an evaluator, a GED teacher, a program secretary, and a part-time driver.

Fifth Ward Enrichment Program. The other clinic-affiliated dropout prevention program is the Fifth Ward Enrichment

Program. This is an in-school, after-school, and summer program for thirty boys who attend a local middle school adjacent to the clinic and are at risk of dropping out. Through early intervention, the program aims to prevent these boys from dropping out of school by instilling a sense of the importance of education. The staff members, all male, act as role models, and through their own behavior try to show the boys that education is important. The staff consists of four full-time staff members—a project director, a social worker, an academic specialist, and an administrative assistant—and two part-time instructors and a part-time clinical psychologist.

Program recruitment occurs in the spring, when soon-to-graduate sixth-grade boys are referred by teachers and guidance counselors to the middle school. During the summer, the boys are enrolled in a program that provides diagnostic testing and some orientation to help the boys prepare for starting middle school in the fall. The program annually enrolls thirty preadolescent boys, mostly twelve or thirteen years old, who are having difficulty with school. Now completing its second year, the program has a waiting list of fifteen or twenty boys.

During the school year, the staff run a daily remedial academic class during school and a two-hour after-school program of academic, therapeutic, and enrichment activities. The after-school activities include field trips, life-skills classes, and workshops sponsored by community leaders. For example, a playwright described the field of drama and had the boys write plays on current issues.

An integral part of the program is reinforcement of good academic and social behavior through a structured behavior management system. Students earn tokens for attending program activities, individual and group counseling sessions, and school classes and for completing their homework assignments; the tokens can be traded in for gifts. Preliminary reports illustrate that the tokens have helped to reduce some school behavior problems. Students who have poor attendance records or are doing poorly academically receive intensive program attention. No student is dropped from the program.

Students are enrolled in the program for only one year. Staff informally keep track of "graduates" during the next school year but have no special services for them. For the second year of the program, the staff are instituting a "godfather" or big-brother type of program, matching program graduates with responsible black male adult volunteers who will encourage their assigned students to apply themselves academically.

The program's success is due in part to the daily contact between staff and students, in part to the close working relationship between its staff and the students' teachers and guidance personnel, who regularly discuss students' academic and personal problems. Program staff are a resource for teachers and parents. They help to educate the teachers about the difficult circumstances in which each boy lives and can assist teachers by following up academic and behavior problems. The program staff encourage the parents to work with their sons, and they sponsor parent-effectiveness courses for them.

Funding

The clinic was launched with two major multiyear foundation grants totaling nearly $1.5 million. Both foundations had built phase-out plans into the grants, intending the clinic to achieve institutionalized self-sufficiency. As a result, the UAC is currently discussing permanent institutionalization with the Hermann Hospital Estate and the University of Texas Medical School. In addition to the annual income from the foundation grants, some income is received from government sources: $5,000 from Medicaid reimbursements and $20,000 from Title XX family planning service reimbursements. Space and utilities are provided by the school district.

The Fifth Ward Enrichment Program is funded primarily by a $134,000 grant from the Hogg Foundation. The TEAM II program's direct funding consists of a $465,000 grant from the Texas Department of Human Services and 133 contributed subsidized job positions.

Evaluation

The clinic maintains records on different aspects of the operations (for example, number of clients served, number of visits, number of contacts, number and types of services provided); however, no comprehensive impact analysis or program evaluation has been undertaken, nor is any planned for the clinic or the TEAM II program. The enrichment program is being evaluated by the Hogg Foundation. Although final results are not yet available, preliminary results show marked improvement in students' attendance, grades, and classroom behavior. There are plans to do a follow-up evaluation in a few years to document the long-term effect of the program.

Although no information exists on the effectiveness of these two dropout prevention and service programs, both are serving critical student populations. The clinic has played a unique role in identifying the service needs of these two groups and in providing supplementary resources for the programs' designs.

Adolescent Primary Health Care Clinic

Program Components

- Free year-round health clinic, easily accessible
- Comprehensive remediation and employment-preparation services for teen mothers
- Dropout prevention program for preadolescent boys
- Clinic program serving as focal point for assessing youth problems

Program Inputs and Outcomes

- Target population: Middle and high school students attending nine schools in a severely depressed area of Houston; teen mothers; high-risk preadolescent boys
- Costs: $300 per student served in the clinic; $2,500 per teen mother in the training program; $4,500 per student in the Fifth Ward Enrichment Program
- Outcomes: Not determined

5

Comprehensive School-Affiliated Programs: Targeting Those at Greatest Risk

Many dropouts exhibit poor attendance and academic performance before quitting school. Several programs have been designed to address early manifestations of these problems intensively, in the hope that these students can be retained through academic assistance, employment preparation, and supportive services. The three programs described in this section illustrate comprehensive high school programs for potential dropouts. All three combine extensive attention to basic-skills remediation and good school attendance with an emphasis on the relation between education and future economic security. They vary in their approach to employment preparation, job training, and supportive counseling.

The first, the Job Readiness Program, is a ninth- through twelfth-grade minischool that is being piloted in two Chicago high schools. It is jointly sponsored by Chicago United, a nonprofit business organization, and the Chicago public schools. Targeted ninth-grade students, whose past academic failures and poor reading scores suggest that they are potential dropouts, are enrolled in a vocationally oriented school within a school. Throughout their high school years, their academic course work emphasizes basic-skills improvement and vocational exploration.

As they progress, they are gradually enrolled in vocational training programs while receiving intensive job readiness training and
counseling support.

The second program, located in rural Massachusetts, is an
alternative high school for dropout-prone and other problem
students referred from neighboring school districts. The Cooperative Federation for Educational Experiences, or Project
COFFEE, provides an intensive and supportive academic and
occupational training program. By extensively soliciting services
and resources from small businesses and major corporations,
particularly the Digital Equipment Corporation, the program
administrators can train students in computer maintenance,
word processing, horticulture and agriculture, distributive education, and building and grounds maintenance, using contributed up-to-date equipment and internships. All the training programs run small businesses.

The third program is an alternative high school located in
a major department store in downtown Atlanta. Rich's Academy is jointly sponsored by the Atlanta public schools and Exodus, Inc., a private, nonprofit education agency. The program
draws on the store's resources to teach students good work habits, to expose them to various vocations, and to pair them with
employees who serve as their mentors. Students attend high
school classes on an unused floor of the store. Atlanta social
service employees are loaned to the program to provide counseling and referral services.

All three programs have made creative use of private-
sector resources for space, equipment, teacher training, and internships for students. All three have expanded their scope and
the employment exposure of their students through extensive
collaborations with small and large employers.

JOB READINESS PROGRAM
Chicago, Illinois

The Job Readiness Program is a cooperative effort between Chicago United and the Chicago public schools to ease
the transition between school and work for inner-city youth.

The Job Readiness Program combines a focus on basic skills with employability training and counseling. It serves 200 youth in each grade of two high schools who perform at least two years below grade level. Summer jobs are provided for those meeting attendance and grade standards. A new group of ninth graders has been enrolled each year since the program began, while services have continued for those already in the program.

With the support of the Edna McConnell Clark Foundation and substantial private-sector in-kind contributions, Chicago United has piloted the program model in two high schools since 1984. The two contrasting settings are a vocational high school with a low dropout rate but a large group of poorly achieving students and a comprehensive high school with a high dropout rate.

Evaluations of the program show improvements in attendance and academic achievement and increases in the youths' positive attitudes about themselves, school, and future employment plans. Significantly greater percentages of participant students than of comparison students were staying in school.

Background

Chicago, like many other northern central cities, is predominantly minority—43 percent black and 17 percent Hispanic —and its public high schools have a high dropout rate. Only 57 percent of almost 30,000 students entering sixty-three high schools ever finish. Yet few opportunities exist for youth who leave school, because youth unemployment rates in Chicago are extremely high. In 1982, 69 percent of black adolescents were unemployed, as were 33 percent of Hispanic and 29 percent of white teens.

The Job Readiness Program was initiated by Chicago United, a nonprofit organization of white and minority business executives who have worked together since 1973 to develop solutions to the city's social problems. In 1983, Chicago United surveyed 7,800 Chicago-area employers to determine the skills that the workplace would require of job seekers in the next decade. Two-thirds of the employers voiced serious concerns about high school graduates' lack of basic skills and employment preparation. Standardized reading test results confirmed these concerns. Entering ninth graders in Chicago had reading scores in the 26th percentile, below 74 percent of youth nationwide.

Acknowledging a shared responsibility, Chicago United became an active partner with the schools in improving the quality of education for disadvantaged minority youth in school and closing the gap between employers' needs and students' academic preparation. After investigating several possibilities, the Chicago United staff developed a basic program model in 1984 to improve the job readiness of potential school dropouts with basic-skill deficiencies, Chicago's least employable youth. The Job Readiness Program model evolved from a joint effort with Chicago public school officials, although a change of superintendents and shifts in organizational structure affected the collaboration.

The Chicago United staff applied for Edna McConnell Clark Foundation funding after attending the foundation's workshops on Jobs for the Disadvantaged, a new program. In 1984, the Clark Foundation began funding the proposed Job Readiness Program and included this model among others to be evaluated by an independent consultant. First-year funding covered initial project planning and piloting as well as data collection on program participants and comparison groups. During the planning period, the Chicago United staff worked closely with the district superintendents and the principals of the two selected schools on program design and implementation.

Two very different high schools were selected for the pilot; both had already begun to address the serious academic and employment preparation deficits among their students. One was Dunbar Vocational High School, a school on the south side of Chicago with an almost entirely black population. Admission to Dunbar was by application; its students therefore came from many parts of the city. The school had formerly been very selective in enrolling students with high academic ability. Recently, in order to serve more students, the school lowered its academic standards and began admitting students who were less well prepared. The other was Farragut Career Academy, a neighborhood high school with equal proportions of black and Hispanic students, reorganized as a career academy when its enrollment doubled after a nearby high school was closed. It serves students from the southwestern part of Chicago.

Farragut Career Academy's students are more disadvantaged economically and educationally than those at Dunbar, although both schools' populations would be classified as disadvantaged. Sixty-two percent of Farragut's students and 35 percent of Dunbar's are enrolled in the schools' free or reduced-price lunch program, for which students are eligible only if their families' income is at or below the federally designated poverty level. Students at both schools perform well below the national average on standardized reading tests: Dunbar students' reading performance is ranked at the 36th percentile and Farragut students' at the 16th percentile. Farragut has a high dropout rate of 55 percent, while Dunbar has a low dropout rate of 28 percent.

Chicago United staff already had a working relationship with Farragut Career Academy through another Chicago United project there, an industry-based career development training center. The Job Readiness Program was tailored to serve the populations each school considered neediest.

Description

The Job Readiness Program reorganizes the existing academic program for targeted students and provides them with additional support in basic-skills improvement, self-esteem counseling, and development of employability skills. In Farragut Career Academy, the program's focus is on dropout prevention; it enrolls students in the ninth grade, when they are most likely to drop out, and provides support services throughout their remaining high school years. At Dunbar Vocational High School, the program provides support and career exposure for low-achieving students in grades 9 through 12.

The program ties together a number of academic and vocational elements to support students while they are in school and to expose them to the world of work (which, it is hoped,

will keep them interested in completing high school). All Job
Readiness students are in the same homerooms and academic
classes. In both schools, Job Readiness students have counseling
and employability skills classes. These class activities range from
participating in a mock application and interview exercise run
by professional personnel managers to visiting companies and
talking with personnel staff.

The program uses a written contract to formalize student
commitment and to encourage parental involvement. Both parents and students are asked to sign a contract in which they
agree to the program's objectives and promise to support the
goals of school attendance and punctuality; parents also agree
to oversee their children's homework. The contracts are reviewed on a quarterly basis along with students' attendance and
grade records. The counselors talk with all the students not
meeting the program objectives and incorporate these problems
into the counseling program. If the student continues to fall
short of the objectives and the parents offer no support, the
program staff will consider dropping the student from the program, as they have done in at least two cases.

Both schools make a concerted effort to involve students' parents beyond the signing of the contract. Parents provide daytime phone numbers where they can be reached if
their child is absent. All materials for parents are printed in
Spanish and English to improve communication. During the
1985–86 school year, four parent-education workshops were
held at Farragut and two at Dunbar; about 30 percent of the
students' parents participated. A Chicago company plans to
sponsor a team-building workshop for parents and teachers in
the program, to be held in a downtown hotel conference center
in the spring of 1987.

The program uses summer and part-time school-year employment opportunities as an incentive to good attendance and
academic work. Students who maintain a 95 percent attendance
rate and pass all their courses are guaranteed summer jobs. The
fourteen- and fifteen-year-old students are given summer work
with nonprofit agencies; those with outstanding performance
receive cash awards of $50 to $100. Students aged sixteen and
older are placed in private-sector jobs. Those students with ex-

cellent summer employer recommendations are referred for the best part-time jobs offered during the school year. All students placed in summer jobs complete an evaluation of their own work. During the school year, as part of the counseling and job readiness instruction, they compare their impressions with those of their employers, who also complete forms evaluating their work.

The two high schools take slightly different approaches to the Job Readiness Program, which are described below.

Dunbar Vocational High School. Dunbar Vocational High School has open enrollment and serves 2,500 students; its academic curriculum is complemented by vocational "shops" emphasizing skill development. During the ninth and tenth grades, students try out different shops and select one as a major for their eleventh- and twelfth-grade years. Students selected for the Job Readiness Program are limited to five training areas: electronics, machine drafting, architectural drafting, graphic arts, and business.

Students are selected for the Job Readiness Program if they perform below grade level and have shown an interest in one of the five shops, which represent the more challenging majors in the school. The program coordinator and the school counselors try to identify which students might have trouble academically in these majors or are at risk of dropping out. In the program's first year, 88 students in grades 9 through 11 were enrolled; in the second year, 125 students in grades 9 through 12 were enrolled.

In addition to attending regular academic and vocational courses, participating students have weekly group counseling on employability skills and individual counseling as needed. Freshmen and sophomore participants have a block schedule for English and math; students with academic difficulties can use a remediation lab.

Students who meet the program requirements are usually offered more desirable jobs than they could get on their own. Wherever possible, students are matched with jobs related to their career interests, and the employers in turn take a strong interest in the students. In the first year, approximately 60 percent of the students were eligible for summer jobs. About half of the juniors performed so well on their summer jobs that they were retained on a part-time basis throughout their senior year. At the end of the second program year, twenty-two of the twenty-six participating seniors were placed in part-time jobs while preparing to graduate. One example is a young man in drafting who is planning a career as a structural engineer because of career counseling he received at the architectural firm where he worked. Another student was assured of a job following graduation that will enable her to attend college.

Farragut Career Academy. At Farragut Career Academy, which has 2,000 students, the Job Readiness Program is tailored as a dropout prevention program. Students are enrolled as ninth graders and remain in the program until they graduate from school or leave for some other reason. The program staff reason that these students need long-term support to make academic improvements.

Program staff select as participants those students who performed poorly in elementary school and are viewed as potential dropouts but are motivated enough to respond to a program such as this. Since almost all of Farragut's incoming students perform below grade level and are potentially eligible for the program, the staff make a concerted effort to identify those at greatest risk of dropping out. To select 100–120 students most in need of the program, they ask eighth-grade teachers and counselors at Farragut's feeder elementary schools to make recommendations, and they review school records to identify incoming freshmen who are reading two years below grade level. They exclude from consideration all special-needs students, such as those with handicaps.

The selected students and their parents are contacted over the summer and invited to participate. Through these interviews, the program staff try to determine which students need the program most and whether the students' parents will provide support. In all, 125 ninth graders were enrolled the first year, and a total of 238 ninth and tenth graders were enrolled the second year.

The Job Readiness Program at Farragut Career Academy

is structured as a school within a school. All participating students are scheduled together for their academic and elective courses. Each Job Readiness student is enrolled in five major classes instead of four, the usual course load. In addition to English (in which they are block-scheduled for the program), science, math, and physical education, they also have a daily vocational survey class and a daily class in employability training and guidance, taught by a program counselor.

When program students become juniors and seniors, they are scheduled for the program on a part-time basis, taking courses in their majors as well. The students are scheduled together for English, where instruction emphasizes basic-skill development. They are also scheduled together for music and art, subjects required of all students. The instruction in these two courses is focused differently for the Job Readiness students; in these classes, the teachers cover the vocational options of these two fields and expose the students to the major art and music institutions in Chicago.

In the vocational survey class, students rotate every ten weeks through four occupational areas—health services, food services, computer services, and business. In each area, students are introduced to career opportunities and the skills and training they require, hear speakers from these fields, visit relevant institutions, and get hands-on or try-out employment experience. The students' daily employability skills and guidance class focuses on self-image development and job readiness skills for success in the work force.

A great deal of emphasis is placed on attendance. Any student who is absent during the first two periods is contacted; if the absence is not accounted for, the parents are notified. Emphasis is also placed on qualifying for and being placed in summer jobs, although the students are ninth and tenth graders.

Participants

In the program's first year, the Job Readiness program served 213 students in two high schools. All 125 of Farragut's participants were ninth graders, and the 88 Dunbar students were drawn from grades 9 through 11. In the second year, 50 ninth graders were enrolled in Dunbar's program and 123 ninth graders in Farragut's. Seventy-five percent of all students in the program the second year were black and the rest were Hispanic; 53 percent were male. Most participants in the second year were from economically disadvantaged families: 60 percent of the Dunbar participants and 90 percent of the Farragut participants were enrolled in their school's free or reduced-price lunch program.

During the program's first summer, 58 percent of the students from Farragut Career Academy and 63 percent of the Dunbar Vocational High School students were placed in summer jobs. The students worked in a wide range of settings, including social service agencies (sixty-two students), hospitals (thirty-nine), grocery stores (twenty-three), and banks (fourteen).

Most of the first-year students continued in the program's second year. Just 7 percent of the Farragut participants and none of the Dunbar students had dropped out of school by the end of the second year.

Staffing and Administration

The program staff consists of one coordinator in each school, a full-time counselor at Farragut Career Academy, a part-time counselor at Dunbar Vocational High School, and a job developer and a project director who work out of Chicago United.

A steering committee oversees the two programs; it includes the project director, both principals, and business people from corporations, utility companies, and hospitals. This committee reviews the Job Readiness Program plan, seeks job placement opportunities, and will be involved in the program's replication process. Each training program—the five vocational areas at Dunbar and the four vocational survey areas at Farragut —has a private-sector advisory committee that reviews the curriculum, visits the classrooms, and checks the skills training and the equipment.

Each school's program operates independently within the

school. The school principals support the programs by allocating instructional staff for the participating students. The project director keeps the field superintendent of all Chicago public high schools abreast of the program's development and progress; the superintendent intends to begin replicating the program soon. Generally, the project director serves as the liaison to the Chicago public schools for the Jobs Task Force of Chicago United. She played a key role in developing the program design, supervises the program staff, and recruits the business representatives.

To provide summer jobs for program participants aged sixteen and older, Chicago United collaborates with five other business organizations and Chicago's Office of Employment and Training to generate summer job opportunities in the private sector. Through a grant from the Mobil Foundation, Chicago United has provided summer jobs placements in nonprofit agencies for younger students.

The Clark Foundation provides technical assistance for the program staff, including periodic workshops on such topics as program needs, job development, curriculum design, and integrating employability skills into course work.

Funding

The Job Readiness Program is supported primarily by a direct grant from the Edna McConnell Clark Foundation and by extensive in-kind contributions from the schools and the private sector. The Clark Foundation provided $30,000 for planning and program development, $148,000 for the program's first year, and $178,000 for the program's second year. Future Clark Foundation funding of this program will be reduced to encourage local district institutionalization.

In addition to the program funding, the Clark Foundation gave an annual $5,000 grant to each of the two school principals to be spent at his or her discretion, not necessarily for the Job Readiness Program. At Dunbar, the principal used the funds to buy software for the remediation lab; at Farragut, the principal bought a computer for attendance tracking and furniture for

the child-care center. This discretionary money is an added incentive for the schools to participate and to compensate for any
extra work involved in having the program. The schools in turn
donate program space, administrative services, and other school
resources necessary for the program's operation.

The private sector is actively involved in this program
through Chicago United's encouragement and the summer jobs
program. Their in-kind contributions are usually channeled
through Chicago United. Dozens of businesses have donated
school supplies, ranging from pencils and paper to a computer
remediation lab at Dunbar Vocational High School. A number
of computers were donated, and one company staffed a computer class at Farragut Career Academy. Corporations have also
provided speakers and training for program staff and have hosted
students on field trips. Personnel department staff from different companies have organized mock application and interview
sessions for students in the program. Students were even taken
to a stockholders' meeting and attended an opera as the guests
of private companies.

Evaluation

Although the program is only in its second year, the first-
year and mid-second-year findings on participant outcomes are
quite favorable. For each school, program staff and an independent evaluator selected a comparison group to be tracked along
with the participating students. The comparison groups (totaling 329 students in both schools) were matched to the participating students by school, grade, race or ethnicity, sex, and
their previous year's grades. A review of their standardized test
performance showed that the math and reading scores of the
first-year comparison students and program students at Dunbar
were similar before the program began; among the Farragut
students, however, the program group started out with significantly higher reading and math test scores than the comparison group.

At the end of the program's first year and in the middle
of the second year, the Job Readiness students had better at-

tendance and grades than the comparison students; the disparity increased the longer the students were with the program. By the middle of the program's second year, first-year participants (now sophomores) at Farragut had raised their grade point averages from 1.2 to 1.4 (on a four-point scale), while the comparison group's average remained at 1.1. The participants' attendance increased from 91 to 98 percent while the comparison group's attendance dropped from 89 to 79 percent between the end of freshman year and the middle of sophomore year.

Dunbar Vocational High School program students showed similar, although less dramatic, gains in grade point averages and attendance between the end of the first year and the middle of the second. Participating students' grade point averages improved from 1.6 at the end of the first year to 1.8 by the middle of the next, while the comparison group's grade point averages increased slightly, from 1.4 to 1.5. Dunbar participants showed similar improvements in their attendance. By the middle of the second year, they had a 96 percent average attendance rate, while the comparison students averaged only 91 percent.

More dramatic program gains were made in school retention rates. By the end of the program's second year, only 7 percent of the Farragut participants had dropped out of school, while 32 percent of the comparison students had dropped out. None of the Dunbar participants had dropped out, unlike 13 percent of the comparison students.

At the beginning and the end of the program's first year, participating students were surveyed on their views about education and their future. More Farragut Career Academy students in the second survey said that they planned to graduate than in the first. Both Farragut and Dunbar participants were more likely to plan on a job or post–high school training and to feel positive about school and themselves than they had been at the beginning of the program. The majority of the students rated the program favorably and particularly liked the field trips, speakers, and career exploration activities.

The first-year evaluation cautioned that the program was ambitious in trying to serve so many students so soon. But the report's author thought the first academic and attendance results were extremely positive, as was the program's success in placing students in summer jobs. These preliminary results seem to indicate that the program is doing a good job of encouraging students to come to school and to apply themselves academically, especially among the Farragut students, who were originally more likely than the Dunbar students to drop out. The long-term success of the program in both schools will be measured by the participants' graduation rates and by their career paths in contrast to those of the comparison groups.

If the program is able to fulfill its early promise and prove its effectiveness in helping a greater percentage of students to graduate, it should have a strong future. Chicago United is committed to maintaining the program in the two schools in which it is functioning and would like to replicate it elsewhere. The staff are currently trying to replace the Clark Foundation funds with state funds for dropout prevention and with other grants. The program is already being replicated in Chicago; another high school near Farragut Career Academy has developed a program modeled on the Job Readiness Program and has obtained outside funding to support it.

The program has also been successful in forging a collaboration between businesses and the schools. The staff have enhanced the vocational exposure of their students with a wide variety of business resources. Using speakers and field trips sponsored by local businesses as well as contributions of equipment and summer jobs.

Job Readiness Program

Program Components

- Comprehensive ninth- through twelfth-grade program for dropout-prone youth
- Focused academic program with basic-skills remediation
- Summer job incentives for good attendance and academic performance
- World-of-work exposure

Program Inputs and Outcomes

- Target population: 400–500 low-achieving high school students
- Costs: $340–490 per student for support staff; in-kind private sector contributions; in-kind school contributions
- Outcomes: Reduced school dropout rate; improved attendance and academic achievement; improved attitudes about self, school, and post–high school plans

PROJECT COFFEE
Oxford, Massachusetts

The Cooperative Federation for Educational Experiences —Project COFFEE— is a regional alternative school located in Oxford, Massachusetts, with satellites in the neighboring towns of Auburn and Webster. A six-year-old program, Project COFFEE provides instruction and occupational training for about 120 students referred from sixteen neighboring school districts. The program is sponsored by the Oxford public schools in partnership with several high-tech businesses and industries, most notably the Digital Equipment Corporation. Through a combination of program components—academic instruction emphasizing basic skills, preemployment training, educational internships, vocational and personal counseling, and a physical education program emphasizing recreational activities—potential youth dropouts participate in alternative learning and job training.

Students who are doing poorly academically or behaviorally in their own high school are referred to Project COFFEE, where most stay to earn their high school diplomas. The program's goal is to improve students' academic performance, reduce their absenteeism, and train them for entry-level employment. To this end, the program emphasizes preemployment training, interpersonal skills, and decision-making skills. Students in the program have made significant gains in reading, language, and math achievement test scores; first-year students have consistently shown improvements in school attendance.

Background

Project COFFEE serves a rural, economically depressed area of southern Massachusetts. The sixteen school districts in the region have a combined student population of 40,000. The annual student dropout rate for the region is 3 to 4 percent, down from 10 to 12 percent several years ago.

In 1979, the superintendent of the Oxford public schools called area superintendents together to plan a program for potential dropouts. Only two responded; nevertheless, they formed a task force and developed an occupational education program, which was to be funded by federal special education money that had recently become available. The program combined special-education and vocational education funds, which had never been done in Massachusetts. It was formally designed, funded, and implemented with the substantial assistance of a local teacher education center and a career education consortium. Project COFFEE began as a carpentry program for twenty-five students referred from three school districts.

Federal vocational education funding was available for only three years, after which the local districts were required to pick up the program. The districts were able to get this funding extended for two more years, but the program's future became uncertain when Massachusetts legislation limited state support of local programs in 1982. In July 1985, new federal requirements made vocational education funding available on the condition that local districts matched the amount of federal funds.

From the beginning, the Oxford public schools superintendent wanted the project to focus on training students for jobs in growing fields. He solicited support from Massachusetts-based computer companies, recognizing that public funding was too limited to establish a high-tech training program. After approaching a number of companies, the superintendent persuaded the Digital Equipment Corporation to become COFFEE's corporate partner in 1980. Since then, Digital has provided over $2 million in computer hardware and software, teacher training, and program consultation, as well as educational internships for students. Project COFFEE staff have also obtained in-kind contributions from other area companies and developed partnerships with small local businesses. By 1985, sixteen school districts were sharing this alternative education program, referring potential youth dropouts at a cost to the district of $3,000 per student plus transportation.

Description

Project COFFEE is housed in two small attached buildings behind Oxford High School, with satellite classes in Auburn and Webster high schools. Classes are held from 7:45 A.M. to 12:15 P.M. and cover five periods, with a ten-minute midmorning break. Students are scheduled for three academic courses and two hours of occupational training each day. The program covers grades 8 through 12; most students are enrolled in the upper grades. The students are divided into groups of ten on the basis of age and occupational interests and they stay with the same group throughout the program in order to develop peer-group relationships. Each student is given an individual education plan that describes his or her specific goals in social, academic, and occupational areas.

Students receive instruction in four academic areas—reading, math, science, and social studies. Each student has two academic teachers who outline the week's course work. Instruction is provided individually or, occasionally, in groups; students work from their own folders of assignments for each subject. The teachers carefully track each student's progress, making daily reports that are summarized weekly on academics and attendance. Those students with advanced academic performance and interest may enroll in classes at the nearby high school, although few do.

In addition to their academic classes, students have a weekly preemployment education class. This class covers job-search techniques, completing applications and preparing résumés, and interview skills, with emphasis on communication and interpersonal skills. Students are also scheduled for two hours of computer-assisted instruction per week in their weakest subject and are required to view one classic book video each week. Students are scheduled for one hour of physical education per week; the instruction emphasizes leisure-time activities and enables students to develop self-confidence and trust in their peers. Activities include bowling, ice skating, golf, and canoeing, using local recreational facilities.

Instructional time is set aside each week for students to meet with social service providers and business and industry representatives. An on-site counselor runs weekly group-counseling sessions with all program students. She also orients new students to Project COFFEE and coordinates additional support services for program participants, such as probation or psychiatric care.

The program provides free transportation for students to and from school, to their occupational programs, and to their internship sites, if necessary. While no meals are provided, students can buy their breakfast before school. All 120 Project COFFEE students come to the Oxford site each morning. The forty students who attend the occupational training programs at Webster and Auburn are later taken by van to those sites.

The program emphasizes occupational training. Students enroll in one of five occupational training programs: computer maintenance and repair, word processing, horticulture and agriculture, distributive education, and building and grounds maintenance. With the exception of the building and grounds program, all occupational programs operate, in part, as small businesses. Students are assigned to an occupational training program on the basis of their interests and their performance on the Occupational Preference Survey.

The word-processing training program is located in Oxford High School. The classroom is set up like an office; each student has a desk, an electric typewriter, and an in-out basket, all donated by the GTE Sylvania Corporation. In this course, students learn typing, word processing, spreadsheet preparation, bookkeeping, and accounting. The program instructor has begun to develop a typing center business, in which students complete job orders such as maintaining mailing lists for local businesses, city government, and the schools. Currently, the students have five business accounts. In addition, three students are scheduled for internships at local schools or at the Digital Equipment Corporation.

A large classroom in the Oxford alternative school site houses the computer-repair program. The instructor, trained as a certified technician by the Digital Equipment Corporation, teaches students to diagnose and repair computer equipment. At the school site, students operate a computer-repair service for fourteen contracting school districts; they repair about 100 machines a year, with a three- to five-day turnaround time. In the past two years, eleven students have become skilled enough to participate in a twelve-week internship at the Digital Equipment Corporation.

In the horticulture and agriculture program, students learn up-to-date methods of running a solar greenhouse and a small farm. They operate the greenhouse on the high school grounds and through it run seasonal plant sales. Students also work on a local farm, maintain school grounds and other civic facilities as a community service, and give local elementary-school children lessons on planting. Students also work for pet stores, landscape companies, nurseries, vegetable farms, and the county horticultural show.

The buildings and grounds maintenance program at the Oxford and Webster high schools provides students with rudimentary training in carpentry, plumbing, electrical wiring, masonry, painting, and landscaping, with an emphasis on current technologies, such as energy conservation. The students rehabilitated a concrete building that is now used as extra classroom space. Off-campus internships include placements with Digital's grounds maintenance department, a local lumber company, and contractors. This program is trying to develop its own small business in building and selling such items as garden sheds, picnic tables, doghouses, and picket fences.

In the distributive education program at Auburn High School, students have their own customized silk-screening and printing service. Local high school student councils contract with the service to print T-shirts and banners. Students manage the company, learning all aspects of running a retail business.

Occupational instructors arrange student internships or

limited-skills training placements with local businesses and industries. Students with advanced occupational and socialization skills are scheduled for limited unpaid internships on a half-day, alternate-day, or alternate-week basis at their instructor's recommendation. The instructor maintains contact with the on-site supervisor, who in turn must submit weekly reports rating the student's attendance, productivity, cooperation, work performance, and willingness to learn. The supervisor's report is followed up in the student's occupational instruction at school. Students cannot go to their internship site without coming to school first. The employers can hire the students as part-time employees after school, but they cannot pay them for the time they work as interns during school hours.

Participants

The sixteen area school districts refer a student to the program if he or she is failing courses, truant, or otherwise having trouble. School staff or parents may request a team evaluation of a problem student, which includes a psychological assessment (according to the state's special-education requirements) and may conclude with a recommendation for an alternative program, such as Project COFFEE. Students may request placement in the program as well.

Students enrolling in Project COFFEE take a battery of tests, including the Occupational Preference Survey and the California Achievement Test. The scores are used to prepare each student's individual education plan.

Typically, 80 percent of the students are enrolled by the first day of school, having participated the year before or having been referred at the end of the prior school year. The rest are referred during the year, usually at the end of each quarter. Students are enrolled in the program on a first-come, first-served basis. To ensure placement for their student referrals, individual school districts can become program members by buying ten slots at $3,000 per slot. All other student referrals, from nonmember schools and from member schools that have filled their purchased slots, are accepted in order. Occasional exceptions are made, such as for juvenile-court referrals.

Entering students often have academic problems; many perform two years below grade level in reading and math. Many also have family and personal problems that can interfere with schooling, such as being in foster care or in a residential program. Almost all students enrolled in the program in 1984 had previously been involved with guidance and special-education services: 68 percent had had at least one experience with the juvenile court system, 74 percent had had psychological intervention, and 57 percent had received social service assistance.

In 1985, 115 students from grades 8 through 12 were enrolled in Project COFFEE. Almost all were white and non-Hispanic, and about two-thirds were male. The largest proportion, 35 percent, were in tenth grade, 26 percent were in eighth or ninth grade, and the rest were in eleventh or twelfth grade.

Attendance and academic performance are strongly emphasized in the program. Monthly attendance reports on all students are sent to the special-education directors of the sending school districts. If students are absent, the staff call them at home. Those absent five times meet with the program director to review their goals. When a student has missed eight days of school, his or her parents are contacted. After twelve absences, the program staff meet with the special-education director of the sending school district to review the options.

Discipline is reinforced by sending a student to an on-site suspension program, the "time-out" room, rather than suspending him or her. If necessary, students can ask to go there to "cool off." While there, students write out contracts pertaining to the incident and are tutored in their class work.

The program has a ten-week marking period, and students' progress is reviewed every five weeks. Students failing after five weeks cannot continue their off-site occupational training or internships until they have made up their academic work. If a student is doing poorly academically, the teachers meet with the student's parents and staff from the sending school district and try to do crisis intervention or other counseling to find out the cause. Often, teachers find that personal problems are the cause of poor performance.

A student with poor attendance or poor academic performance meets with the project staff to develop a contract for improvement. If the poor performance continues, the sending school is notified and the district team meeting reconvenes to rewrite the student's educational plan and to discuss alternative placements. This has been necessary for less than 1 percent of the Project COFFEE students.

Annually, program staff and sending school staff meet with students to review how they are doing and whether they would prefer to return to their sending school. The special-education director from the sending schools will try to bring back only those students who have met the attendance, behavior, and achievement exit criteria determined by their school district. Since there is a limited number of spaces for students in the program, those who are doing well may be encouraged to return to their high school to make room for others.

To complete the program successfully, the students must meet all graduation requirements of their sending school, including credit and attendance requirements. Since 1979, 85 percent of the students entering Project COFFEE have obtained high school diplomas or have been mainstreamed back into their sending high school. Until 1985, about 40 percent of the students returned to their sending schools. Since then, only 5 percent have returned, the staff having concluded that it is better to keep them in a program where they are successful and happy. As new occupation-related learning experiences have been added, students have preferred to remain in the program, and they and their parents usually request that they not be mainstreamed. About 15 percent of the students are unsuccessful in Project COFFEE; they are terminated from the program and placed elsewhere, drop out of school, or leave the program for personal reasons.

Staffing and Administration

Project COFFEE is overseen by a project director and staffed by six academic teachers, six occupational training teachers, a counselor, and four instructional aides; all report directly to the superintendent of the Oxford public schools. An academic and an occupational teacher are paired to team-teach the physical education activities; in all courses, each teacher works with ten students per class period. Teachers from the Oxford public schools volunteer for assignment to Project COFFEE. The severe problems of the youth in this program and the close teacher-student relationship are very demanding for the teachers and represent the greatest staff problem.

The program has an advisory board of nine people from labor, business, industry, higher education, and the community at large. The program's partnership with business and industry has been a critical component of its success. Everything from state-of-the-art computer equipment to staff training and consultant services has been contributed by the Digital Equipment Corporation. While a few other corporations and businesses have supported Project COFFEE, Digital is the key corporate partner, supplying internship experiences for all occupational areas.

Funding

The 1985–86 school budget for Project COFFEE was $420,000; the cost per pupil was $3,000, excluding transportation costs for students in three sites. This is about 20 percent higher than the per-pupil cost of $2,400 for students in regular day programs. Each school district pays the full cost, including transportation costs, for each student it places in the program; thirteen districts use local school district appropriations and three districts use federal special-education funds.

Revenues earned by students in the small businesses they run are used to offset equipment and supplies costs for each occupational area. The computer-repair business generates about $2,500 and the silk-screening operation of the distributive education program about $4,000; the other training programs generate nominal income.

Evaluation

In 1981, Project COFFEE submitted evidence of its effectiveness to the Joint Dissemination Review Panel (a federal panel that determines whether a program is effective in meeting its stated purpose on the basis of objective evidence). The evaluation demonstrated statistically significant basic-skills improvement; acquisition of entry-level job skills; improved self-concept; and decreased absenteeism. At the time of the evaluation, 59 percent of the Project COFFEE students were still in the program or had been mainstreamed. Eighteen percent had graduated, joined the military, or gone on to full-time employment in their training field. The remaining 23 percent had moved, had dropped out of school, or had been placed in a more restrictive environment.

With the Joint Dissemination Review Panel's approval, Project COFFEE qualified as a developer/demonstrator project with the federal National Diffusion Network. This qualification generated funding for the staff to document the program's curriculum and administrative policies and to help other school districts adopt the program model. By 1985, Project COFFEE had received inquiries from forty-four states and several other countries and had been replicated in at least eight school districts across the country.

In 1986, Project COFFEE again submitted evidence to demonstrate its continued effectiveness and was validated by the panel. The program demonstrated its effectiveness over three years in increasing students' academic performance, decreasing absenteeism, and improving students' employability. The second approval provided continued funding for dissemination efforts.

In Project COFFEE's more recent report on its effectiveness, preprogram and postprogram achievement test data were available for 104 program students, representing 39 percent of those enrolled between the 1982-83 and 1984-85 school years. (It was unclear why postprogram data were unavailable for a larger portion of the enrolled students, but the preprogram test scores of this group were similar to those of all enrolled students.) These students showed statistically significant gains in reading and language scale scores for all three program years and for math in two of the three years. These gains, while very positive, must be reviewed with caution, because of the small number of students.

First-year Project COFFEE students in all three years had

statistically significant gains in attendance from the previous school year, on the basis of the attendance records of 79 percent of the enrolled students. In 1985, first-year students' attendance improved from 87 to 91 percent. Six months after their 1985 graduation from Project COFFEE, twenty-four students were interviewed about their current employment and educational status. Ninety-two percent had graduated from high school and 70 percent were employed, most in jobs related to their training.

The project has received additional citations and honors. In 1982, it was awarded a Presidential Citation as a successful industry-education partnership and was named one of ten National Lighthouse Sites by the Department of Education for its efforts to help school districts use technology effectively in education. In 1983, the project was certified by the Massachusetts State Department of Education as a "Promising Practice" program in working with special-needs students.

The program's overall success is attributed to the self-contained alternative environment and the integration of vocational training with hands-on experience and academics. Because they team-teach, the occupational and academic instructors reinforce each other's work with the students. Other attributes of success are the low student-teacher ratio, which allows a close and supportive relationship to develop, and the affective and counseling components of the program, including those built into the transportation service, the in-school suspension program, and the physical education activities. What makes the program stand out, however, is its partnership with major corporations and small businesses. This partnership strengthens the vocational training and expands the learning and postprogram employment opportunities for the student participants.

Project COFFEE

Program Components

- Comprehensive alternative vocational program for referred potential dropouts
- Alternative-school setting

- Integration of academics, occupational training, physical education, and counseling
- Entry-level job training and work experience in a growth field
- School-business partnership

Program Inputs and Outcomes

- Target population: Potential dropouts with social and academic problems from sixteen regional school districts
- Costs: $3,000 per student, excluding transportation; internship sites; business support
- Outcomes: Lower dropout rate; improved attendance; improved basic-skills performance

RICH'S ACADEMY
Atlanta, Georgia

Rich's Academy is an alternative high school serving 110 near-dropouts and former dropouts, nearly all of whom are black and poor. Located in Rich's, a major downtown Atlanta department store, the academy is one of the Cities-in-Schools (CIS) programs administered by Exodus, Inc., an Atlanta-based nonprofit organization. Formed in 1971, Exodus is a partnership of business, professional, and lay people; its primary goal is to reduce the number of high school dropouts in Atlanta. Through its academies and alternative school programs, Exodus works closely with the Atlanta public schools, the city and county governments, community service agencies, and the private sector. This public-private collaboration is designed to bring social services and other resources to needy students at the alternative educational sites. The CIS program is also closely linked to the private sector through the generous efforts of the president of Rich's department store, who provides substantial in-kind assistance and resources to the program.

The primary objectives of Rich's Academy are to motivate students to attend school regularly and to enable them to acquire the confidence and skills that will help them obtain high school diplomas. The academy's methods blend the traditional and the innovative. The teachers are part of the Atlanta public school system; the academic courses follow system guidelines, and discipline is strict but not harsh. Because they are in a department store, the students—many of whom have parents who have never worked—are exposed daily to the routines and rigors of the workplace. They have the opportunity to develop personal relationships with assigned store employees and to be employed part-time and sometimes full-time. Staff on loan from the Atlanta Department of Social Services provide supportive counseling and referrals.

The message that Rich's Academy tries to convey in all activities—academic, counseling, social, and cultural—is that there is no substitute for self-esteem. This philosophy, a comprehensive human services program, a committed staff, and the unique relationship to Rich's department store are the ingredients for an effective school for dropouts and would-be dropouts. This is demonstrated by the program's 70 percent graduation rate and 15 percent rate of return to regular high schools as well as by students' gains in achievement test scores.

Background

The Atlanta school system has faced a number of challenges over the past decade. The school population shrank from a peak of over 113,000 in the 1967-68 school year to less than 72,000 in 1980-81. The school desegregation battles in the early 1970s ended with most of the white students leaving the city schools; the percentage of white students dropped from 40 percent in the 1967-68 school year to 9 percent in 1980-81. Many black students from affluent backgrounds are also said to have left the school system during this period. As a result, 80 percent of the students currently enrolled in the Atlanta public schools are reportedly from families classified as poor, and 90 percent are black. Yet through the extensive efforts of the superintendent and district staff, Atlanta's schools have begun to improve steadily in recent years. Gains have been made in math and reading achievement test scores. The annual dropout rate in Atlanta's public schools has fallen from 5 percent in

1972-73 (representing a cumulative dropout rate of 18 percent) to 4 percent in 1984-85 (a cumulative rate of 15 percent).

Rich's is one of three "street academies," alternative programs that Exodus administers through its CIS program in Atlanta. Street academies were pioneered in Harlem storefronts in the 1960s. Committed young men worked closely with disaffected youth to provide "caring discipline" while tutoring them; these methods proved effective at educating poor inner-city youth. In the late 1960s, this approach was transplanted to six cities, Atlanta among them, by a pilot program run through the U.S. Post Office. When the Post Office program was phased out in 1972, Exodus provided the organizational and financial support needed to continue the Atlanta street academies.

The CIS program was developed in 1974 through the joint efforts of Exodus and the Atlanta public school system to improve the coordination and delivery of educational, social, and other resources at the academies themselves. The CIS model was considered so effective that in 1977 a national program was started and the model was replicated around the country.

The academy was established in Rich's department store in 1982-83. The president of Rich's wanted to take on a specific project to help disadvantaged youth in Atlanta. Besides providing space in the downtown store, he has made himself and his staff available to support the school's operations.

Description

On Monday mornings at 8:40, students, teachers, human services staff, and the project director gather in a large room on the sixth floor of the Rich's building in what was once the store's bakery and is now the hub of Rich's Academy. No old-fashioned assembly, this is a personal development session, at which students who have done particularly well in some area during the past week are singled out for praise by the adults present and are applauded by everyone. No step forward in a student's progress is too small to be noted: if a shy student began to participate in class or went for a job interview, or if a student who has had trouble with vocabulary mastered a difficult word, the accomplishment is duly noted and celebrated. Students are invited to participate; for example, they might give feedback on school activities, analyze a poem, or comment on world news. These meetings are held to wipe away Monday morning blues, motivate the students to embrace the week of learning ahead, and, perhaps most important, to heighten the students' sense of self-esteem. Such a session illustrates the way the academy endeavors to get in touch with its students, spurring them to become engaged and think positively about themselves.

Tuesdays through Fridays start off with four "families," or groups of students, meeting from 8:30 to 8:50 A.M. in smaller rooms off the large room. These groups of twenty or thirty students are selected at random and stay together throughout the year. One academic and one nonacademic member of the staff, one male and one female, are assigned to each "family." After attendance is taken, the group becomes, in effect, a group-counseling session in which academic and attitudinal matters are addressed. The matters to be discussed in these sessions are chosen and strategies for their resolution are developed at Tuesday afternoon staff meetings. When it is decided that a student's problem is personal or for some other reason is not appropriate for group attention, the problem is taken up in a private session with the student by the two staff members assigned to his or her "family."

Four fifty-minute classes in reading and English, math, science, and social studies fill up the morning, with a ten-minute midmorning break. The goal of the classes is to provide each student with enough academic credits to graduate and the ability to pass the state-required basic-skills test. Students are assigned to one of three class levels according to their last scores on the basic-skills test, which is administered twice a year; the class levels are coded in an effort to protect the students' self-image.

Following a fifty-minute break for lunch, two afternoon classes are held from 1:10 to 2:50 P.M. Students performing below grade level are required to attend remedial education classes in reading and math. The others have a range of electives to choose from: career education, home economics, teen parenting, public speaking, computer science, performing arts, writing, and geography. From 2:50 to 3:00 P.M., the "family" gathers again to make certain that everyone is still in attendance.

"Extended day," which runs from 3 to 6 P.M., is a time for after-school activities (such as performing arts) and tutoring for students who are failing subjects or just want extra help. Rich's employees, whose time is donated by the store, and other volunteers supplement the staff's activities during this period. At the end of the day, the project director waits by the elevator to hand out free transportation tokens, words of encouragement, and, if necessary, gentle but firm admonishments.

Consistent with its theme of enhancing student self-esteem, the academy has developed and integrated many other supportive components into the school. Counseling is not, strictly speaking, considered a separate program activity but pervades all activities at Rich's. The program director explains that "everyone on staff serves as counselor," and that staff members strive to deal with problems as they come up. The director, who sees himself as a sort of head counselor, is constantly being called upon by students seeking advice. Staff frequently call students aside for a gentle but firm talk that appears to be a hallmark of the academy's style—chiding a girl for slippage in attitude or encouraging a shy boy not to miss an upcoming field trip.

When the staff believe that a student's problems are beyond their capacity to help, the program director and the Exodus staff at Rich's—a social service coordinator and a counselor and special-events coordinator—make referrals to outside agencies for social and other services or work with several counselors from outside agencies who come to Rich's regularly. A specialist in substance abuse prevention employed by Fulton County visits the academy twice a week. An art therapy teacher, also employed by a Fulton County agency, works with the students once a week. Counselors from the county health department come to the program twice a week to work with students who have mental and physical problems.

In the 1983–84 school year, according to Exodus reports,

the staff gave social service assistance to Rich's students twenty-six times (help with financial problems, housing, clothing, food, day care, AFDC, and food stamps) and made ninety-eight additional social service contacts and referrals for them. During the same year, the staff also delivered health services 123 times (assistance with family planning, sex education, alcohol and drug abuse, and other health-related issues) and made an additional 561 contacts and referrals for health services. They also made thirty-one contacts to provide legal assistance and fifteen contacts to provide probation monitoring for academy students in trouble with the law. The academy provides career counseling and holds a career day during which representatives of twenty-five businesses and professions come to the school.

Volunteers play a vital role in the program. Approximately fifteen give their time during any given week. Over forty-five volunteers from Rich's department store were involved in CIS programs in 1983-84. Rich's employees volunteer to participate in an "Adopt-a-Friend" program, in which they provide personal and academic support for their assigned students. Students visit the different departments of the store (such as the advertising division) and learn firsthand what store employees do. Among other things, these visits give a concrete basis to the relationship between volunteers and academy students. The volunteers tutor the students during the extended day, receiving instruction and direction from the compensatory education teachers at the academy. Volunteers also work with the students on special activities, such as performing arts.

The academy's location in Rich's also offers students some unique opportunities to learn about work and discipline. If the students arrive at school late, they are sent home. Like store employees, they must abide by the rules of the workplace and come to school at a designated time.

During the 1985-86 school year, Rich's store hired six students to work part-time; three other students were placed in part-time jobs elsewhere. Every summer, Rich's department store hires up to thirty academy students. Students are exposed to various aspects of running a large department store: keeping inventory, stocking shelves, and working with customers.

Academy staff members visit the home of each student once or twice during the school year to acquaint the parents or guardians with the academy and to encourage their interest in the child's attendance and academic progress; during 1983-84, the CIS reported eighty-eight visits to the homes of academy students. The visits also help staff to understand better the problems facing each student.

Parents come frequently to the academy for conferences; 434 parent conferences took place during 1983-84. The academy organized a parent-teacher organization in 1985-86, which forty parents and guardians joined. Meetings every two months give parents an opportunity to be involved in the school.

The academy includes other cultural and social enrichment components in its programs. Field trips are structured around curriculum subjects. Students and staff are trained as mediators as part of the national Neighborhood Justice Center program. A leadership program draws selected students together regularly to discuss career goals and to enhance self-esteem. The academy is also a member of the Special Audiences program, which brings professional musicians and other artists to the school. After a performance, students have an analytical discussion and perform themselves, singing or reciting poetry. Again, the emphasis is on the development of confidence and a strong sense of self.

Participants

Rich's Academy, according to its own publications, seeks to serve students who are "unable or unwilling to attend a regular high school program." To be admitted into Rich's Academy, a student must be between fourteen and twenty-one years of age, reside within the boundaries of the Atlanta public school system (most students are from one region of the district), and supply a transcript and withdrawal statement from the last school attended and an immunization report. Students are enrolled on a first-come, first-served basis. As part of enrollment, each new student completes an achievement test, the results of which are used to make the student's education plan. Enrollment is limited by the size of the facility; an informal waiting list is kept so that if a student drops out or is terminated, another is enrolled.

In 1985-86, 110 students were enrolled in the program. An estimated 60 percent were former dropouts, 90 percent were from families on welfare, and 50 percent were from broken homes. Sixty-five of these students were girls; all but three were black. The average age was sixteen. Most students are referred to the program by the regular high schools or, less often, by the courts. Some are referred by their friends or by other Rich's Academy students.

Although Rich's Academy has a point system of discipline that can lead to termination—expulsion—it is rarely used. Students are more often asked to leave because of poor attitude (not taking an interest in classes) or poor attendance and punctuality. In 1985-86, about 10 percent of the students quit or were asked to leave. After sitting out a term, these students are generally allowed to rematriculate. Attendance overall is good; in 1983-84, the students averaged an 87 percent attendance rate.

Available data and interviews indicated success in placing graduates in jobs immediately following graduation. All twenty-five graduates in 1985 went on to either postsecondary education or jobs. The CIS reported in 1983-84 that eighteen of twenty-five graduates (sixteen of whom had been dropouts) had jobs by June 30, and that seventeen had plans for attending postsecondary institutions. Program staff estimated that twenty-five students would graduate in 1986; by April, job placements or training opportunities had already been found for about a dozen of them.

Staffing and Administration

The academy's full-time staff consists of six teachers, a social service coordinator, a counselor and special-events coordinator, a registrar, and the project director. Three part-time counselors are donated by community agencies. The six teachers are from the Atlanta public school system and have volunteered to teach at Rich's. They are interviewed and selected by the project director. The student-teacher ratio is between 15:1 and 20:1.

The project director oversees the day-to-day operations of the academy. He reports to Exodus formally each month, but informal daily contact is maintained and the relationship is harmonious.

Exodus, through its CIS program, in turn makes periodic evaluation reports to the Atlanta public schools system, which is highly supportive of the academies and takes great pride in them. As the sponsoring organization, Exodus provides administrative support and funding to Rich's Academy. It employs the social service staff, including the registrar, negotiates arrangements with the agencies providing the social service support, and works with the program director in providing staff development and training.

The Atlanta public school system provides all instructional staff and administrative oversight. The office of job placement of the Atlanta public schools oversees all CIS programs, including Rich's Academy. Its director has been a strong advocate within the school system for continued and expanded support of the program. Diplomas are granted to the graduates of Rich's Academy by Archer High School, a conventional public high school with which the academy was affiliated before moving to the store. Academy students can use the athletic facilities at Archer and can play on its teams.

Officials at Rich's department store, particularly its president, have taken a strong and active interest in the program. In addition to contributing space, the store permits its employees to volunteer time during working hours to tutor students and help with after-school activities. The store's president is strongly committed to helping high-risk youth. His leadership has encouraged the support of other private businesses; as a leading Atlanta businessman, he has spearheaded fund-raising activities on behalf of Rich's Academy and other programs.

Funding

The program is supported by a mixture of funding resources and in-kind contributions. The school system, with local education funds, provides the instructional staff and materials.

The space and related expenses are contributed by Rich's department store. Exodus, through its own private fund-raising, supports the social service staff, except those loaned from city and county agencies. The annual program expenditures are approximately $285,000 for on-site staff, including teachers and Exodus administrative staff, representing an average cost of $2,600 for each of the 110 students served.

Evaluation

The impact of Rich's Academy is demonstrated in the achievement test scores of its students and, ultimately, in their high school graduation rates. California Achievement Test results show a gain of approximately one grade level annually in reading and math. On the average, 70 percent of the students graduate with a high school diploma awarded by Archer High School and with a Rich's Academy certificate. Another 15 percent return to a conventional high school or some other academic program; 15 percent have negative termination—that is, they are expelled or drop out.

Students interviewed at Rich's Academy were enthusiastic in their praise of the program. They saw it as a place where they could fit in and grow. One student said, "I was always getting into fights at my old high school." At Rich's, he is part of the leadership program. These students expressed a good deal of confidence and had concrete plans for the future. Two students, one of whom was a mother, were planning to go on to college.

Rich's Academy has many strengths—its clear goals and structure, its connection with the schools and network of support services, its strong parent organizations and connections with Rich's department store, its attempt to bring self-esteem to its students, and its excellent attendance and graduation statistics. The leadership at Rich's Academy appears to be strong, the teachers competent and committed, the conceptual framework correct, the political and administrative pieces firmly in place, and the students very happy to be there. The program model has received nationwide attention and is beginning to be replicated elsewhere; Foley's department store in Houston is planning to institute a similar school.

Rich's Academy

Program Components

- Comprehensive alternative school for referred potential dropouts
- Department-store setting
- Alternative school environment
- Full high school program
- Strong emphasis on self-confidence
- Contributed social services support staff

Program Inputs and Outcomes

- Target population: Dropouts and other at-risk youth in Atlanta public school system
- Costs: $2,600 per student; contributed space; volunteer assistance
- Outcomes: 85 percent complete high school; all graduates go on to jobs or postsecondary school

6

Redirecting the Dropout: Preparing Out-of-School Youth for Gainful Employment

~~~~~~

Substantial numbers of students quit school each year, and very few programs exist to help them complete their education once they have left. It is unrealistic to assume that many will later return to high school and earn a diploma; public schools rarely try to recruit students who have dropped out.

This chapter describes two nonschool programs specifically designed to recruit and educate youth dropouts. Both offer "no-frills" academic instruction, emphasizing basic-skills remediation and GED preparation. Both combine instruction with personal counseling and employment orientation, although the focus remains on developing basic skills and passing the GED. Both have flexible entry and exit schedules. While both programs take a locally focused approach to delivering services, they differ substantially in origins and funding.

The first is the Alternative Schools Network in Chicago. Thirty-five alternative schools and youth centers provide income-eligible sixteen- to twenty-one-year-olds with educational services to help them obtain a GED or a high school diploma. This network has received funding for and implemented the Comprehensive Competencies Program in twenty agencies. This is a computerized, self-paced basic-skills instructional program that can be tailored to the individual student and combined with other program services.

The second program comprises the privately operated Educational Clinics located in seven counties in Washington State. The clinics' sole purpose is to recruit youth dropouts and to assist them in completing their GED or returning to a regular high school. The program is available primarily to youth dropouts who have been out of school a minimum of thirty days. The program is funded by the state education agency, which reimburses the clinics for every student-hour of instruction delivered. The agency uses a performance-based contract that determines the clinics' future funding on the basis of how cost-effective they are and the degree to which the clinics target hard-to-educate students.

ALTERNATIVE SCHOOLS NETWORK
Chicago, Illinois

A network of thirty-five community-based alternative schools and youth centers in Chicago provide a structured program of education, employment preparation, job training, and counseling for youth dropouts throughout inner-city neighborhoods. As the Alternative Schools Network, these nonprofit agencies do joint fund-raising for their program and state and local education advocacy work on behalf of their constituency. These local agencies serve approximately 2,000 youth dropouts annually, assisting them in getting a high school diploma, returning to public high school, or obtaining a GED.

Since 1984, the agencies have raised private and government funds through their central network office to implement the Comprehensive Competencies Program. This is an individualized, competency-based, self-paced teaching system that has been particularly effective for teaching basic skills. This program has become the core of educational services for youth dropouts, most of whom are poor. The program is supported by substantial Job Training Partnership Act funding and locally raised funds.

Background

With a public high school dropout rate estimated at 53 percent, the Chicago school system is losing approximately 14,000 students per year. In spite of this acute educational problem, the school system has only recently begun to sponsor new programs. The few dropout-prevention and service programs currently established are insufficient for all who need them. The education and training services available through the thirty-five agency affiliates of the Alternative Schools Network are the only substantial and widely available learning alternative for youth dropouts in Chicago.

These community-based agencies formally established the Alternative Schools Network in 1973 in order to share ideas on educational methods and programs. In 1975, the network received its first grant funding, and since then it has taken advantage of prevailing funding resources to establish education, employment and training, and social service programs among its affiliates.

Description

The thirty-five community-based agencies comprise twenty-three alternative schools with programs leading to a high school diploma and twelve youth service centers. All share common goals: providing young dropouts with an opportunity to learn in a supportive environment and offering services to help modify the causes of truancy and dropping out, to remediate skill deficiencies, and to assist youth in the transition into working life. The agencies serve over 2,000 young dropouts annually.

These goals are reflected in each agency's program. The instructional program is individually designed and self-paced, linking the curriculum to everyday experiences and students' specific needs. Support services offer students counseling and referral to other social services. Almost all students receive thirty to forty hours of job readiness instruction, including job-seeking assistance, on-the-job support, and placement in a job training program. Some agencies offer in-house skills training in computer programming, word processing, carpentry, and retail sales training.

Upon entry into the alternative high schools, students are given a number of tests that assess their weaknesses in specific skills. The results are used to develop an individual educational plan. Each school offers instructional sequences in English, math, science, social studies, career education, and health—all the subjects needed to meet Illinois state requirements for a high school diploma. The schools resemble mini–high schools, with a broad curriculum and student activities such as sports.

Some alternative schools are licensed to award diplomas; others grant diplomas through an affiliated public high school. All the schools' programs are small, serving 25 to 200 students. They maintain small classes; the average teacher-student ratio is 1:8. While class organizational patterns and schedules vary considerably among the schools, all run full-day and full-school-year programs. Students remain in the alternative schools an average of one or two years.

In contrast to the alternative schools, the youth centers operate on an open-entry, open-exit basis. They provide individual instruction based on diagnostic test results. Dropouts often come to the centers for employment and support services; academic or GED classes are usually a secondary concern. The centers offer activities such as vocational and employment counseling, job readiness training, job clubs, job referral and placement, and internships along with basic-skills remediation. Those who wish to upgrade their academic skills stay as long as they need.

The centers are open five days a week, six to nine hours per day; a few centers have shorter schedules. Typically, students attend half-day sessions three to five times each week, receiving two hours of academic instruction and one hour of job readiness instruction, including daily work in a learning resource room, if the center has one. Attendance is emphasized to help students develop responsible behavior. Students are enrolled in GED-preparation classes for an average of five to six months. All agencies emphasize basic-skills remediation through individual and group course work and tutoring provided by volunteers. The Comprehensive Competencies Program is becoming the primary educational method used by the agencies to help students improve their basic skills and to complete their education.

In February 1984, the Alternative Schools Network became the second organization in the country to implement the Comprehensive Competencies Program (CCP). The CCP is a nationally distributed competency-based instructional program developed by the Remediation and Training Institute in Washington, D.C. It is a self-paced instruction system based on sequenced workbooks and computer software. With this system, students can prepare for the GED, improve basic skills, and achieve competency in various areas of job readiness and occupational interest. Instruction is hierarchically organized toward specific learning objectives. Corresponding tests assess students' mastery of each objective, providing feedback and pinpointing problem areas. A critical component of the program is an automated management system that tracks individual students' progress.

Over a two-year period, twenty network-affiliated community agencies added CCP learning centers with the support of locally allocated federal job training funds. Every agency's center is equipped with between five and twelve computers as well as printers and related peripheral equipment. About half the youth dropouts served by the network-affiliated agencies have received CCP instruction.

A typical CCP has a fully operational learning resource room equipped with the CCP's academic and functional components and staffed with one full-time instructor and two center aides. The learning resource room is open at least eight hours each day; students attend for one to three hours daily and focus on upgrading their skills in specific areas. Students using the CCP curriculum must demonstrate 80 percent mastery of assigned topics before moving on to their next assignments. Student progress is reassessed after every hundred hours of instruction and upon exit from the program.

The network recently completed an evaluation of the agencies' use of the CCP. Through extensive interviews, it identified strengths and concerns associated with the implementation and current operation of the program. The primary finding was that the CCP program had not been adopted or integrated uniformly among the twenty centers. Agencies wanted to be flexible in using the software for instruction and had problems in getting software, skilled staff, and hardware. When the CCP was first introduced, program directors were enthusiastic about its usefulness for students' GED preparation and remedial education; they saw that individual programming could enhance the existing curriculum. The directors found that the CCP was an efficient instructional tool, gave students a chance to explore several subjects, and improved attendance and self-esteem. Yet they also found that it took them and their staff a long time to learn to use the system and to fulfill recording requirements. This was exacerbated by staff turnover and difficulties in learning to integrate the CCP with other programs and to administer it. Students also had initial difficulties in learning to use the CCP; part of this was due to anxiety about computers and testing. Some students were unable to work on their own, were inattentive, and did not apply themselves to the program.

Participants

The thirty-five network-affiliated agencies serve youth dropouts who have a broad range of academic, economic, and social needs. According to Network staff, 95 percent of these students are public school dropouts; most are eligible, on the basis of their economic status, for federally supported job training programs. The majority perform three years below grade level in basic skills and about half have had contact with the juvenile justice system. While program eligibility varies among agencies, most students are between fourteen and twenty-one years of age. In all, the agencies serve over 2,000 youth dropouts annually.

Students are referred to the agencies by other agencies, schools, friends, and word of mouth. The alternative schools and youth centers do their own recruitment and intake.

Most of the information available on the youth dropouts

served is limited to those who use the CCP instruction—about half the student population. In March 1986, the average enrollment at the twenty centers with CCP resources was 1,365 students, or an average of about seventy per site. Fifty-six percent of the students were female; 57 percent were black, 20 percent Hispanic, 11 percent white, and the rest Asian and Native American.

Each agency sets its own graduation standards. Most of the alternative schools require students to achieve a ninth-grade reading level, pass a state test on the U.S. Constitution, and accumulate sufficient course credits. At the youth centers, students successfully complete the program when they pass the GED test and get a job. About 60 to 70 percent of the students who enroll in the alternative schools or youth centers stay and complete their GED or obtain a high school diploma.

Centers set their own standards for disciplining students. Students are rarely dropped from the program, and then only in extreme cases, such as when a student is dealing drugs or involves the center in local gangs' turf battles.

Staffing and Administration

In joining together as the Alternative Schools Network, the thirty-five alternative schools and youth centers, along with fifteen nonprofit preschools and elementary schools, established an administrative and support structure with an elected board of directors. To qualify as a member in the network, a community agency must have nonprofit incorporation in the state of Illinois and must be self-governing in all respects.

The network has a strong relationship with the office of the mayor of Chicago, which oversees the city's federal job training funds. Although no formal ties exist between the network and the Chicago board of education, many of the network's alternative schools work closely with nearby public schools.

The network is staffed by an executive director, who was one of the organization's founders, and by an educational and technical assistance unit staffed by a director and two program associates, all of whom are trained in CCP methods by the Remediation Training Institute. There is also a job training unit, which has its own director and four program staff members for intake, vouchering, and program liaison, and a social service unit with a director and an assistant.

In representing fifty centers, the network's staff carries out three program functions: fund-raising, public advocacy, and program support and resource development. By serving as a central fiscal agent, the network is able to use its clout and obtain large grant support for the affiliates.

Funding

The programs and services run by the affiliated schools and youth centers are supported by a mixture of agency and network-generated funds and by monies from the state and city governments, businesses, and foundations. Each agency itself raises $60,000 to $100,000 annually. The network's own budget for the 1985–86 program year totaled approximately $1.9 million in federal, state, and foundation funds. Major funding components include two federal job training grants (the smaller portion of which is for the Pre-Employment Training Program), a Title XX social services contract (for support services at twelve sites), an Illinois state education grant (for teachers and support services at seventeen sites), and support from various local and national foundations.

Over 75 percent of the network's budget is distributed equally among the twenty neighborhood learning centers that use the CCP instruction. The network's program committee makes all final allocation decisions. The CCP consumes a large part of the expenses; Remediation and Training Institute management services, training, and consumable supplies cost $12,000 per year per site (or a total of $240,000), and computer leasing from local vendors costs another $100,000 per year. Central administrative costs incurred by the network were about $440,000 in 1985-86.

Evaluation

Student performance in the CCP is constantly monitored as part of the management information system. Yet the student progress and outcome data from all centers have not been aggregated to provide an overall picture. Therefore, no comprehensive evaluation information on the program is available.

The information that is available is limited to students using the CCP instructional system. By the third quarter of 1986, information was available on 589 students who had completed the CCP that year. Their average reading score when entering the program was at the seventh-grade level; 11 percent read below the fifth-grade level, 38 percent between the fifth- and seventh-grade levels, 28 percent between the seventh- and ninth-grade levels, and the rest above ninth-grade level. Their average gain in reading was 1.6 grade levels and their average gain in math was 1.1 grade levels during the eight to ten months they spent in the program.

The network's future plans include the addition of five to ten new CCP sites under the network's umbrella and the expansion—in both numbers of youth served and the scope of services provided to them—of the network-sponsored dropout programs funded under the state education program.

The network illustrates an effective way for community-based organizations to target the needs of school dropouts in their area by working together to raise funds and implement a focused program.

Alternative Schools Network

Program Components

- Collective of alternative schools and GED-preparation programs for out-of-school youth
- Neighborhood learning centers
- Open-entry, open-exit programs at some sites
- Comprehensive Competencies Program for self-paced basic-skills and employment preparation instruction

Program Inputs and Outcomes

- Target population: Neighborhood school dropouts
- Costs: Not calculated
- Outcomes: 60–70 percent high school/GED completion rate

EDUCATIONAL CLINICS
Washington State

In accordance with a 1977 state law, Washington State funds nine Educational Clinics designed to provide short-term educational intervention services to public school dropouts. In addition to instruction in basic academic skills, the clinics provide employment orientation, motivational development, and support services. One for-profit and eight nonprofit clinics serve 1,750 youth dropouts annually throughout Washington.

The clinics are performance-oriented, focusing on academic gains and the course the student will pursue after leaving the clinic (generally, returning to school or completing the GED exam and going on to employment or further education). A medical type of approach has been adopted by this program—for example, the terms *diagnose, prescribe,* and *treat* are used. Each clinic applicant begins by completing a standardized achievement test and an interview, through which the student and clinic staff work out goals for the student's stay at the clinic. The student is tested again when he or she leaves. The program's philosophy is that individual services can motivate dropouts to change behavior, overcome personal problems, and acquire the basic skills that are prerequisite to success in employment and educational endeavors.

Funded since 1978 by Washington State, the clinics operate under contract with the state education agency. The clinics are reimbursed only for time actually spent in testing and instructing students. Detailed performance standards provide the clinics' incentives to be cost-effective; they serve each student for an average of $636. Sixty-six percent of the students successfully complete the program by obtaining a GED, transferring into another educational program, or obtaining employment.

The state legislature estimated in 1986 that the existing clinics had served 13 percent of each year's 10,500 school dropouts in the state's seven most populous counties in 1983-84 and 1984-85. The clinics are not considered alternative public schools and do not offer academic credit or issue diplomas. They have been closely scrutinized by the State's education community and are subject to rigorous reporting requirements. Two other states, Colorado and California, have implemented similar state-funded programs.

Background

The educational clinic model began in the late 1960s when the founder of Educational Clinics, Inc. (ECI), a for-profit organization, ran a "War on Poverty" training program, primarily for adults on public assistance. He concluded that a world-of-work training approach, with its emphasis on the procedural side of training and job placement, was insufficient if the trainees lacked basic academic and social skills. He found similar skill deficiencies in the high school–age youth who came to the training centers looking for tutoring. He concluded that most of these out-of-school youth wanted an education, but not necessarily through the public schools. Drawing upon this training experience, he and the current executive vice-president of ECI developed the educational clinic concept during 1974-75 by running a pilot program in Everett, Washington, a predominantly working-class city near Seattle. Then as now their fundamental principle was that without basic education, help with personal problems, and employment orientation, young people will not be able to find and keep jobs.

Armed with the track record acquired during the pilot phase in Everett, and with a clinic still in operation, ECI began lobbying for state legislative support in 1976. In 1977, the Educational Clinic Act was approved by the Washington state legislature, signed into law by the governor, and given a one-year appropriation of $425,000. ECI and three nonprofit agencies were certified by the state board of education and began operating clinic programs with state funds in July 1978. In 1979, the program was given $1 million for the next two years. Since then, five other state-funded clinics have opened, and three non-funded clinics were certified in the spring of 1985. These educational clinics currently serve youth dropouts in the seven most populous counties in the state.

The educational clinics are only one of several efforts to reduce the statewide dropout rate. Almost 15,000 students dropped out of school in 1982-83, according to a study by the Office of the Superintendent of Public Instruction (OSPI), the state education agency. Twenty-five percent of all entering ninth graders will not graduate from high school four years later. Educators and public officials throughout Washington have said that the dropout problem is worsening. Currently, the state funds a number of alternative public school programs and dropout prevention projects, in addition to the educational clinics, all of which serve potential as well as actual school dropouts.

Description

The goal of the clinics is to serve dropouts by individually diagnosing instructional needs and setting a course that allows the student to proceed at his or her own pace toward a "positive activity" at exit—either returning to public school or passing the GED test and going on to work or further education.

The enabling legislation sets out the basic components of the clinics. It specifies that basic skills be taught by state-certified teachers and the courses this entails, that specific attention be paid to improving student motivation and employment orientation, and that each student be given individual goals and an instruction plan. Clear and concise, the legislation prohibits vocational instruction and "courses nonessential to the accrediting of the common schools" (Washington State Legislature, 1978). If a clinic fails to provide adequate instruction in basic skills, it loses its certification. The legislation spells out who is eligible for clinic services. With some exceptions, it restricts eligibility to adolescents under twenty years of age who quit high school at least thirty days before enrolling in the program.

The legislation requires clinics to administer a test approved by the OSPI to students when they begin and conclude the program. The Peabody Individual Achievement Test (PIAT) was selected; it measures the extent to which a student has mastered reading, spelling, mathematics, and general information. If a student applying for entry into a clinic tests below the high school proficiency level and meets the other eligibility standards, he or she is admitted to the clinic on a space-available basis. The clinic staff use the PIAT results, and sometimes other standardized achievement tests, to develop a student's instruction plan. Clinic staff may also refer a student to social workers, probation officers, or school counselors if other kinds of diagnosis are needed.

Together, the clinic staff and the student review the test results and discuss personal, family, and other problems, such as why the student left school. The student's prior school is requested to provide proof of enrollment and verification of the withdrawal date. Academic goals (such as returning to school or passing the GED), employment goals, and social goals (such as improving personal and family relationships or curtailing drug and alcohol use) are agreed upon and become the student's prescription for clinic participation. The diagnostic interview process sets high but realistic expectations for each student; it also lets students know that the clinic staff care about their success. Thereafter, student and clinic staff meet regularly to assess progress and, when appropriate, to modify goals and objectives.

Prescribed basic-skills courses—math, speech, reading and composition, science, history, literature, and political science—are taught individually or in small groups in which students are usually grouped by ability. Course materials tend to be eclectic, drawn from surplus textbooks, magazines and newspapers, and materials of the staff's own making. About half the clinics provide computerized instruction.

Each clinic organizes its instructional program differently. At the Everett clinic, five teachers and one tutor work with eighty-five students grouped into four academic classes of fifteen to twenty and a tutorial class for students with special problems. Students are grouped by ability for math and reading.

Normally, the Everett clinic has four hours of classes between 8:30 A.M. and 12:45 P.M. Students move up from one group to the next on the basis of a mastery test taken whenever the student feels ready. An example of a smaller clinic is the United Indians of All Tribes Foundation clinic in Seattle. This clinic has two teachers, including one who acts as clinic administrator, a tutor, and fifteen students. Students are grouped by age and ability to give them the sense of being in a regular school. The classes run from 9 A.M. to 3 P.M. and use computerized instruction.

Clinics employ a range of techniques to motivate students academically and personally. Critical thinking and values clarification are an integral part of the curriculum. The diagnostic approach used by the clinics helps students recognize their strengths and weaknesses and gives them realistic goals to attain. To encourage responsible behavior, the clinic staff may have students sign weekly contracts that outline expectations for attendance, academic work, and behavior. Clinic staff also encourage students academically by having them sit for the portion of the GED exam they are most likely to pass. Students who pass one section are highly likely to pass the entire exam eventually.

Clinic staff also recognize that helping students cope with their personal problems is another way to motivate them. Some clinics, such as the one in Everett, rely largely on the close relationship between teacher and student for personal counseling. However, true to the medical analogy, the staff do not hesitate to call on a specialist when problems outside their scope, such as drug or alcohol abuse, occur. Other clinics rely more on the regular involvement of outside counselors. For example, the United Indians of All Tribes Foundation clinic has weekly group-counseling sessions, known as "Adventures in Attitude," that are tailored to the needs of its largely Native American student body. The clinic also schedules outside cultural and recreational activities to encourage students to take pride in their heritage.

Good attendance is critical to clinic operations, because the clinics are paid only for the hours that the students actually attend. Students are contacted if they do not show up for classes. Staff also follow up home problems that may keep students away from school. Some clinics use financial incentives to encourage good attendance: a modest sum, perhaps ten dollars, is banked weekly for each student, who in turn loses two dollars for each day missed. Several clinics are able to provide free lunches and transportation services for their students, in cooperation with the local schools, to promote attendance.

Clinics offer students employment orientation through workshops, guest speakers from various professions, assistance with résumé writing, and released time for job interviews. Clinics also instruct students in survival skills, such as using checking accounts and budgeting and managing money. The Yakima clinic provides twice-weekly classes in preemployment training and self-esteem development. A "reentry program" has been instituted at the Everett clinic that prepares students returning to school to cope with a large, impersonal bureaucracy that cannot give students the same personal attention they had at the clinic.

The clinics can enroll students for up to 135 days, but they can plan for no more than 75 days. If a student needs to remain in the program for more than 75 days, the staff must file an extension request with the state education agency explaining why the work was not completed and how it will be completed in the next 60 days. If a student needs instructional assistance beyond the 135th day, the clinic may "carry" a student at its own expense.

Students attend clinics for an average of thirty-three days. Although each student has an individual instructional program, the per-student average is 8 hours of instruction one-on-one with a teacher, 6.5 hours in a group of two to five students, and 108 hours of instruction in a group of six or more.

In 1978, the state regulations were modified to permit clinic students to return to the public system at the grade level they would have been in had they not dropped out. To do so, the dropout must have attended the clinic for at least ninety hours. In addition, the student must be performing at grade level. To graduate, the reenrolled student must put in at least three out of four years of high school, including a full senior year.

Participants

The Educational Clinic Act states that only "eligible common school dropouts" shall qualify for reimbursement by the state. This includes youth thirteen through nineteen years of age who are unable to pass a high school equivalency exam and who have been out of school for at least thirty days, those referred by their school, and those who have been suspended or expelled. Clinics recruit students through occasional advertising, referrals from the courts, community agencies, local schools, and other students. At the Everett clinic, for example, over 70 percent of the students had heard about the clinic by word of mouth; 11 percent were referred by schools, and the remainder came from the courts and community agencies. Clinics serving highly disenfranchised populations, such as Native Americans, recruit some students on the streets where they congregate.

In 1984–85, the nine clinics served 1,757 students. The average clinic student that year was 16.2 years old at entry, had left school after 9.4 grades, was 2.7 years behind grade level, and had been out of school for 4.2 months. Clinic students come from diverse backgrounds. State officials estimate that roughly three-quarters of the clinic students are white and the rest are Native American, Hispanic, or black. Equal numbers of males and females attend the clinics. Most are from economically disadvantaged families. In 1984–85, 23 percent of the clinic students were from families on welfare, 76 percent did not live with both natural parents, and only 12 percent were employed when they enrolled. In addition, 24 percent of the students were on probation.

Students are rarely dismissed from the program; if they are, it is usually for criminal activities, such as selling drugs. Students with poor attendance or inappropriate behavior are counseled and sometimes suspended, but they are not usually dropped from the program.

Students interviewed at random at the Everett clinic were

open and articulate in their enthusiasm for the program. One said it was "for kids who can't make it in school." Another said he "didn't get enough attention in school." A third said, "The teachers are our friends; they treat us equally." Of twelve students interviewed, seven had been expelled from school; five said they would not be allowed to return.

While much more reserved, the Native American students interviewed at the United Indians of All Tribes Foundation clinic seemed no less appreciative of its efforts. The program director reported that the students' families often had a transient life-style; many of the students suffered from cultural dislocation, and several had drug and alcohol problems.

Most students successfully complete the program. Sixty-six percent of the students who attended clinics in 1985 left for a "constructive activity": 30 percent reentered high school, 24 percent passed their GED test, 9 percent took full-time jobs, 7 percent obtained part-time jobs, and 2 percent each enrolled in higher education and vocational education programs (some students began more than one activity). The remaining 34 percent were looking into school or employment, were institutionalized, or were doing nothing. Clinic staff are more likely to counsel younger students to return to a regular school; such an option is less realistic for older students.

Staffing and Administration

While all the clinics provide the same type of service, they differ widely in size, clientele, and type of sponsoring agency. Nine organizations currently operate educational clinics at sixteen sites. ECI, the for-profit entity, has 175 students in attendance at three sites on any given day. The eight nonprofit organizations run clinic programs at thirteen sites with a total of 180–190 students attending daily. Three of the nine organizations run the educational clinics as their principal function; one, an approved private school, can grant diplomas. The other six are multipurpose agencies that operate training, cultural, social service counseling, recreational, and other programs in addition to the clinic.

Clinics serve as few as eight or as many as one hundred students at one time. Three serve mainly Native American students. Clinics are usually in cities, but they also serve substantial numbers of suburban and rural youth. The clinics operate year-round, although enrollment and waiting lists decline in the summer. While these obviously different circumstances mean some variation in how the clinics function, the program model is very adaptable.

Each clinic administrator hires state-certified teachers to work year-round. Average student-teacher ratios range from 8:1 at the smallest clinic to 20:1 at the largest. ECI has a board of directors and an active advisory board drawn largely from the business community. The six nonprofit clinics affiliated with multipurpose agencies are integrated into their sponsoring organizations, through which they receive in-kind support, such as rent-free space and policy guidance. The nine educational clinics have formed a statewide association that meets occasionally and works with state legislative staff to ensure continued state funding.

The Community Education/Educational Clinic Section in the Vocational, Technical, and Adult Education Services Division of the OSPI administers the clinic program. It monitors programs, approves monthly payment vouchers, makes payments for the clinics' testing and instructional services, and allocates state funds among the clinics. It recommends certification of new clinics and recertification of existing ones to the state board of education on a three-year cycle.

Funding

The state support for clinics in 1978-79, the first year of operations, was $425,000. After that, state funding was allocated biennially. In 1979-1981 and 1981-1983, $1 million was allocated per funding cycle for education clinic services. In 1983-1985, funding was increased to $1.85 million; in 1985-1987, it was increased to $2.33 million.

Each year, clinics contract with the OSPI to serve a projected number of students that is based on quarterly student estimates. The clinics submit monthly vouchers to the OSPI for reimbursement. While these vouchers cannot total more than the quarterly projections, each clinic's funding can be adjusted between quarters as staff perceive changes in service delivery. During the last quarter, the OSPI staff may distribute unspent funds among clinics.

Clinics are reimbursed at a statutory per-student hourly rate according to type of service and student-teacher ratio: $50 for diagnostic testing, $16 for individual instruction, $10 for classes with two to five students, and $5 for classes over six. The students may not be charged a fee.

The clinics' average per-student reimbursement has declined by 19 percent between 1980 and 1985. In 1979-80, 893 students were served at a per-student cost of $784. This dropped steadily to an average cost of $636 in 1984-85, when 1,757 students were served. In the latter year, the clinics' per-student reimbursement ranged from $461 to $976, reflecting differences in student-teacher ratios (larger clinics can more frequently provide large-group instruction, which is far less costly than individualized or small-group instruction) and in the proportion of students who need extensive instruction.

The clinics' funding is allocated according to past funding and clinic performance as evaluated by OSPI's superior performance formula. Unique in its specificity and completeness, this performance formula rates the clinics on the basis of:

- Student achievement, measured by PIAT testing and the percentage of students engaged in positive activities after leaving the program
- A determination of difficulty-to-educate, based on the mean number of months students have been out of school, the percentage on welfare, the percentage not living with parents, and the mean number of years behind class
- The average reimbursement per student.

If a clinic's performance score is close to the average for all nine clinics (± one standard deviation), its funding is not affected. If the score is more than one standard deviation above average, funding is increased by 10-15 percent. A score more than one standard deviation below average results in a 10-15 percent funding reduction. A very poor performance, two or more standard deviations below average, will end clinic funding altogether. Clinics have occasionally had their funding reduced or increased because of their performance, but no clinic has yet lost funding altogether.

The 1984–85 OSPI superior performance calculations show wide variations in clinic performance and student body: from 56 to 81 percent of the students served that year had finished the program and gained, on the average, from 2.9 to 10.4 achievement points on the standard achievement test. In difficulty-to-educate ratings, from 17 to 56 percent were not living with both parents; the students had been out of school from 1.5 to 13.9 months and were from 1.9 to 3.2 years behind their classes.

These data, along with the clinics' per-student reimbursement rates, were combined in a weighted index score in which ratings ranged from 111 to 180. Clinics receive higher ratings the lower their average student reimbursement (which is in proportion to the number of days students attend and the student-teacher ratio per hour of instruction); the greater the percentage of students who obtain their GED, reenroll in high school, or are employed when they leave the clinics; and the greater the percentage of students who are difficult to serve. Clinics can improve their performance score, and thus their funding, by targeting the hardest-to-serve youth and by providing instruction more efficiently, such as by using large-group rather than individual instruction.

Clinic directors estimate that the state per-student reimbursements represent only 80–90 percent of the actual cost of serving each student. The clinics occasionally raise small amounts of money from individuals, businesses, and foundations and through events such as dinners or bake sales. The nonprofit clinics affiliated with other agencies often receive some in-kind or financial support from their host agency.

Evaluation

The clinic services are monitored and evaluated by three mechanisms: the annual OSPI monitoring, the OSPI superior performance rating, and the biennial State Legislative Budget

Committee evaluations. The OSPI reviews all funded clinics each year as part of the clinic certification process, monitoring the clinics' adherence to the state guidelines and regulations. The outcomes of this review and of the superior performance rating are reflected in each clinic's funding.

The state legislature has required several biennial reports on the clinics' performance and impact since they were first funded in 1978. The legislative budget committee prepares a fiscal impact study and a comparison of the clinics with other educational and institutional alternatives. The four reports prepared since 1978 show the clinics to be a highly effective, low-cost means of serving out-of-school youth.

The 1985 legislative report of cost information for 1982–1984 concluded that the clinics' per-student costs were fairly constant during the two-year period. The report noted that while the legislature wanted the clinics to be compared to alternative schools, their goals, structure, and types of student were too different. The report showed, however, that alternative schools for dropout-prone youth achieve similarly positive outcomes but at a higher cost than clinics. The report concluded that both "clinics and alternative public programs serve legitimate purposes and are worthy of public support" (Legislative Budget Committee, 1985, p. 42).

In 1985, the OSPI prepared a report, at the legislature's request, showing that clinics often serve more dropouts than the state reimburses them for, using supplementary funding sources or operating at a loss. The clinics estimated they would serve 2,408 students with 1985–86 allocations but might serve as many as 4,160, on the basis of their current recruiting, waiting lists, and past experience with unreimbursed service.

The legislative budget committee found that all clinics emphasized returning to school for younger students and obtaining a GED for older students. Full- or part-time employment or entering the military were also counted as positive outcomes for student participants. Between 1980 and 1984, the clinics maintained a high positive termination rate: from 66 to 69 percent of the clinics' students completed the program with one of the above outcomes.

To determine the clinics' long-term effect, the legislative

budget committee conducted a follow-up study of a randomly selected 10 percent of the 1984 students. Six months after leaving the clinics, 62 percent of eighty-six students surveyed were still in constructive activities, just below the 66 percent at the time of leaving the program. The report regarded this finding favorably, concluding: "While there is some drop-off, education clinics appear to have a lasting positive effect on a significant percentage of their students" (Legislative Budget Committee, 1985, p. 3).

In 1984, ECI conducted a more extensive telephone follow-up study of 462 students who had completed the program five years before. Although ECI was able to contact only 178 (39 percent) of the former students, those interviewed were similar to those not interviewed in characteristics at enrollment (age, sex, dropout status, educational status, employment status, and involvement with the welfare or judicial systems). Seventy percent of the 178 students had completed the educational clinic program; the rest had dropped out before finishing. Five years later, 71 percent were employed, in a postsecondary education program, or supported by a spouse.

ECI attempted to obtain similar information on twenty-two people who enrolled in but never attended the educational clinic program, but only nine were found. In age, education, welfare and judicial system status, and dropout status, these nine youth were similar to those who had actually attended. They were found to be doing less well five years later—only 44 percent were employed, in school, or supported by a spouse. But nine youth are too few to serve as a comparison group. ECI's evaluation does demonstrate the program's sustained effect on its students. Without monitoring a similar comparison group, however, it is difficult to ascertain the program's full significance.

A hindrance to the clinics' success in Washington has been the lack of support from the public education community. Some public school officials, thwarted by stiffer requirements for their students, resent the flexibility of the clinic programs, and they do not view preparation for the GED as an appropriate alternative to a high school education. A few officials have resisted accepting a student's achievements in the clinics when the student reenters high school, have not referred eligible students, or have not provided documentation of the students' eligibility for the clinics. State education officials and the Washington Business Roundtable, a group of interested business people, are trying to bridge the gap between the two education communities.

The thorough evaluations of the clinics' operations and impact provide independent evidence of their effectiveness in serving dropouts. For many students, the clinic offers their only means of completing their education. The clear guidelines provided by statute and the performance evaluation appear to make the program model and the state funding formula readily transferable. The clinic model has been replicated in Washington and in other states. Since the first four clinics supported with state funds started in 1978–79, the number of operating clinics has grown to nine and three more certified clinics await funding.

Both Colorado and California have passed state legislation to fund similar programs. California recently awarded nine school districts funds to establish educational clinics themselves or to contract for this service through another agency. Six districts are developing clinics; of the three contracted out, two are being set up by ECI. In 1985, Colorado passed legislation to fund a Second Chance Program. This established six opportunity centers (with six more planned) for youth aged sixteen to twenty-one to work toward a GED or high school diploma through an individualized education plan. The centers are operated by public schools and can accept eligible students regardless of where they were previously enrolled.

Educational Clinics

Program Components

- Local centers for GED preparation and high school reentry for youth dropouts
- Flexible entry and exit policies
- Small classes with basic-skills focus

- Personal and social counseling and referral
- State support

Program Inputs and Outcomes

- Target population: Any public school dropout (aged thirteen to nineteen) who has been out of school at least thirty days or has been referred, suspended, or expelled
- Cost: Per-student reimbursement of $636 in 1984-85; in-kind local agency support
- Outcomes: 66 percent left the program for reentry into school, a GED, employment, or postsecondary education; 62 percent of former students were in constructive activities six months after leaving the program

7

Systemwide Strategies: Reducing the Dropout Rate in Complex Urban School Systems

With over 30 percent of their entering ninth-grade classes likely to drop out, urban school systems are implementing extensive programs to improve their student retention rate. State legislatures are also allocating new funds to address what is primarily an urban problem. The substantial amount of new state and local funding has enabled urban school systems to experiment with different approaches to preventing students from dropping out. One common solution is to add a program to serve the most dropout-prone youth; a few school systems, however, are simultaneously considering ways of restructuring their educational delivery system to respond better to all their students' varied educational needs.

The two efforts summarized here illustrate different assumptions about how to improve school retention. New York City and Los Angeles have the largest school districts in the United States, with high percentages of minority and disadvantaged children. Multimillion-dollar state and local appropriations have given both districts new resources with which to test strategies for keeping more students in school. New York City is focusing on attendance improvement and on school and community collaborations for special dropout prevention programs.

A core set of services target students with the lowest attendance rates on the assumption that they are the most likely to drop out.

Los Angeles, also piloting dropout prevention programs, has funded feeder elementary and junior high schools along with high schools targeted for their high dropout rates. Rather than require the funding to be used for a standard program, as in New York, the school district has given school principals the discretion to tailor program designs to local needs.

As a broader dropout prevention measure, both school systems are also making systematic changes in the management and operations of their schools. New York is requiring all high schools to maintain a low dropout rate and to demonstrate measurable progress toward achieving this and other student performance goals. Los Angeles is reviewing various aspects of the system's structure to determine whether and how they can be changed to expand the educational options for all students.

SYSTEMIC APPROACH TO DROPOUT PREVENTION
New York City

New York City's efforts to reduce its high dropout rate combine two school systemwide strategies. One directs a mix of support services to the secondary school students most likely to drop out, as their poor attendance shows. The other makes middle schools and high schools responsible for the rate at which their students drop out and for the academic performance of their students.

New York City's cumulative dropout rate for high school students was estimated to be 35 percent in 1984–85 and even higher among minority youth. Average daily attendance was 85 percent for middle schools and 79 percent for high schools. With a total student population of over one million and with decentralized elementary and middle schools, it has been difficult for the New York City school system to respond to such a pervasive educational problem promptly and effectively.

Through a series of New York State and New York City

policy decisions on school and student performance standards and appropriations of over $30 million in new program funding to improve student attendance, the New York City school sys- tem has developed a standard approach to reducing its dropout problem. By 1986-87, the ninety-seven middle schools and thirty-six high schools with the lowest attendance rates had comprehensive attendance improvement and dropout preven- tion services for 150 of each school's poorly attending students. The outcomes of these programs and the comparative benefits of the different program designs are being evaluated by the New York City board of education and an external evaluation team.

At the same time, each school with poor student atten- dance, retention, and academic performance is developing a comprehensive school improvement plan to remedy these prob- lems. The New York City board of education has determined that no high schools' dropout rate is to exceed 7.5 percent an- nually. Holding each school accountable and requiring each school's administration and staff to plan comprehensively and to take measures to meet this goal should yield beneficial re- sults.

It is too soon to know whether the system's two-pronged approach to dropout prevention is effective. It appears, how- ever, to be a sensible means of serving the students most in need while prompting schools to improve their educational programs to reduce the need for more dropout prevention services.

Background

The impetus for the new school performance standards came from the New York State Board of Regents (the state board of education) in 1984. The board required that all schools reach at least minimum standards for reading and math test scores and expand the course requirements for their core programs and for graduation.

The state education department followed by creating a school district evaluation and reporting system, the Compre- hensive Assessment Report, to assess student progress in each school. Progress was measured by whether the students in each school attained minimum state reading and math test scores and whether the schools maintained low dropout rates. The state would intervene if schools were found to have unacceptable student progress levels or discriminatory policies and practices. The first review, in 1985, found that 393 New York City public schools were in need of assistance, including 237 elementary schools, 102 middle schools, and 54 high schools.

In 1985-86, the New York City board of education expanded this accountability in several ways. First, the board added student attendance, citywide reading and math test performance, and graduation rates to the performance criteria. Each school was issued a school profile that reported its performance on all criteria.

Second, the board outlined a school improvement plan for schools identified as in need of assistance. For the 1986-87 school year, this plan set measurable objectives for improving performance on each criterion. According to the new minimum performance standards, high schools are not to exceed a 7.5 percent annual dropout rate (representing a 27 percent cumulative dropout rate). For the first time, each high school's success is to be measured in terms of its ability to hold on to its students as well as to meet minimum standards of student test scores and attendance rates. Schools with annual dropout rates higher than 7.5 percent must demonstrate significant progress—at least a 50 percent reduction—within three years. Those not showing measurable improvement after three years would be closed, redesigned, or otherwise restructured.

The school improvement plan required schools needing assistance to use a collaborative, school-based planning process and to stipulate their own measurable objectives in developing a comprehensive school improvement plan. It is up to the individual school to determine the best way to restructure its programs to improve student attendance, retention, and academic performance.

To help schools meet the new minimum standards and to improve school services generally, the New York City school system has outlined a long-range plan for the addition of special services. According to this plan, by the year 2000, all middle schools and high schools are to have a dropout prevention program and a core set of the services currently being piloted under the newly funded attendance improvement and dropout prevention programs. These include attendance services, health services, educational remediation and enrichment, links between school levels, and collaboration with community agencies.

Description

At the same time that the new system of standards and accountability were added to the management and operations of New York City schools, the board of education added a large-scale attendance improvement and dropout prevention program. The program was made possible by city and state funding initiatives that targeted poorly attending students in middle schools and high schools with low attendance rates.

History. In 1984, coinciding with recommendations from the governor and the New York State Board of Regents, the state legislature passed a bill for attendance improvement and dropout prevention. The legislation appropriated $28 million in new state aid to school districts with the lowest attendance rates to fund programs and services for attendance improvement, on the assumption that poorly attending students are the most likely to drop out. Through formula funding, $22.3 million was allocated to New York City.

In the first funding year, confusion existed, especially in New York City, over which age-groups were to be targeted, how much was to be spent on technical equipment rather than staff, and how coordination and community involvement were to be achieved.

For the second year of funding, the 1985-86 school year, the state legislature tightened the regulations by amending the education law to address these questions, while maintaining appropriations at $28 million. At the same time, New York City's chancellor added more specific guidelines on how the funds were to be used in each school and what types of program models were permitted. Six services were to be standard: program facilities, health services, attendance outreach, guidance and counseling services, links between school levels, and alternative school programs. Programs were to target students with excessive absences in middle schools and high schools with high absentee rates.

The second year of state funding coincided with a New York City appropriation of $10 million for additional dropout prevention efforts. The program, known as the Dropout Prevention Program, selected ten high schools with high dropout rates and twenty-nine middle schools to be laboratory schools. Two approaches to service delivery were tested: a case-management approach, in which community-based organizations provide some or all dropout prevention services, and a systemic approach, in which the regular school program incorporates these services into a program for selected students. The city-funded programs were designed to incorporate the same core services used in the state-funded programs.

In 1986, the state legislature amended the program again and increased the funding for New York City by $8 million. Two more types of students were made eligible: pregnant and parenting students and students receiving public assistance and living in hotels or other temporary dwellings. The legislation specified that the plan's measurable performance objectives were the improvement of performance, attendance, and retention. All services were to be coordinated as much as possible with services available through local, state, and federal programs, particularly state compensatory education programs. New York City made additional changes, adding summer planning sessions for the staff, extending services through the summer, developing a pilot middle school program for special-education students and a pilot program for long-term absentees, and adding a jobs component.

Program Design. The state- and city-funded attendance improvement and dropout prevention programs are based on well-known principles for reducing dropout levels. The first is that unexcused student absence is an early sign of trouble. Second, severe attendance problems begin to occur in middle or junior high school. Third, since students leave school for many reasons, a comprehensive program can best address individual needs. Fourth, a number of community-based agencies and city social agencies have resources that can be used to fight the problem. Finally, limited resources can have more impact if they are reserved for those schools and students with the greatest need.

The city- and state-funded programs were implemented in 1985-86 in middle schools and high schools whose attendance rates were at or below the median citywide attendance rate (87 percent in 1982-83). Each school's program was to be funded for three years.

New York City has established common guidelines for the state-funded and city-funded programs that reflect the board of education's perspective on what is needed to improve and maintain student attendance. Six core services are to be fully integrated into a comprehensive program for each student:

1. *Facilitation.* Each school must appoint a regularly licensed teacher to serve as facilitator and give the teacher at least two free periods to track the progress of targeted students, work with the pupil personnel committee, and coordinate the program.
2. *Attendance outreach.* Each school must supplement its existing daily attendance program with outreach services to follow up absent targeted students, including communication with parents by phone or through home visits. Incentives may be used to encourage good attendance. A committee of key school and program officials meets periodically to review attendance.
3. *Health services.* Targeted students are to be given priority for school-based health services provided through the New York City health department. Each school is to make certain that these students are screened for physical and psychological problems that may interfere with their schooling and is to refer students to appropriate services within the school or to other community agencies. This service cannot be funded with dropout prevention funds.
4. *Guidance and counseling services.* Counseling services must

be made available to every targeted student to identify and address individual problems that may cause poor attendance.

5. *School-level links.* Each school must develop strategies to help incoming students make successful adjustments to their new school. Each high school must develop a plan for graduating middle school students from at least three major feeder middle schools, with special attention given to high-risk students. Middle school students in dropout prevention programs will be given the opportunity to enroll in a summer remediation program. To help them in tracking and programming students, high schools will be notified which incoming students were in middle school dropout prevention programs.

6. *Alternative education programs.* The programs must include interesting activities to motivate targeted students. The programs should incorporate basic-skills instruction and individual attention. These are usually in the form of career education instruction or after-school tutoring and enrichment.

The services are to target 150 students with poor attendance who are drawn from a list of eligible students generated by the board of education. In the middle schools, students in the upper two grades who were absent between thirty and seventy-four days the prior school year are targeted; additional criteria are to be used to select students if not all slots are filled. In the high schools, 100 students who were absent at least twenty days in the prior spring term or who were designated as long-term absentees the prior school year and have been absent at least ten days in the first two months of the current school year are selected as the core students. The state-funded programs must have a transitional program for fifty students with the above characteristics and for those who were enrolled in the previous year and have shown improved attendance. Program staff can spend up to $50 per student on incentives.

The city- and state-funded programs are implementing five combinations of the six core components that differ in theme, content, and service delivery. They are (1) SOAR (Student Opportunity, Advancement, and Retention), (2) Strategies, (3) Operation Success, (4) a case-management approach using community organizations to deliver some or all services, and (5) a systemic approach that incorporates the services into the regular school program. A critical feature being tested by these programs is the collaboration between schools and community agencies. The board of education is exploring the benefits of drawing the resources of community agencies into the schools, which may be better equipped to help youth with personal, academic, or social problems that discourage their school attendance and achievement.

The SOAR program, supported with state funds, targets overage ninth graders. It is in use at sixteen high schools that structure the six program components around one of two alternative education strategies: a block program for small groups of students with a daily tutorial period and individual instruction for students who return to school midyear.

The Strategies approach is used by seven high schools and is also funded through the state program. In order to provide the six components, school officials select services from a menu supplied by the board of education and organize these selections around a theme to create a modified minischool program for targeted students. Three high schools using this model contract with community-based organizations for some services, such as counseling and alternative education.

Sixty-eight middle schools have implemented a modification of the Strategies program with state funding. Students with poor attendance in the two upper grades (seventh and eighth or eighth and ninth) are targeted for each school's program. The six core components are not structured as a minischool program as they are in the high schools. The middle schools select from the alternative education components either after-school enrichment or career education, which covers personal development, decision making, career awareness, and business enterprise. By January 1986, the sixty-eight middle schools were serving 11,300 students.

The third approach, a work readiness and experience program called Operation Success, is in use in seven high schools, which in turn contract with a private human services agency, the Federation for Employment and Guidance Services. This program, supported by both the city- and the state-funded dropout prevention programs, offers a range of services to address students' personal and vocational training needs and to encourage them to stay in school. The services include outreach, case management, community service referral, vocational evaluation, skills training, educational internships, and part-time employment. Eligible students are scheduled as needed or interested for individual or group counseling, educational internships, part-time jobs, and skills training at the federation offices. Four of the high schools emphasize the case-management approach to counseling and referral services for their targeted students. In 1985–86, 2,500 students were enrolled in Operation Success, all of whom received at least some counseling and career guidance. Eleven percent had an educational internship, and 16 percent were enrolled in skills training at the federation offices.

Following the collaborative approach to service delivery without the vocational focus, fourteen middle schools have implemented a case-management approach to dropout prevention, drawing on the services of community-based organizations. The schools subcontract with an organization to provide some or all of the six core program components, using their counseling and social service resources. This approach is funded through both the state and city programs.

The final approach is the systemic one, which six high schools and fifteen middle schools have adopted. The school staff draw on a variety of innovative techniques—cluster grades, mentoring and work experience, minischools, extended-day programs, reorganized guidance services, and curriculum improvement—to restructure the basic education program for targeted students. Unlike the Strategies approach, these techniques are not structured around a miniprogram. Three of these high schools purchase case-management services from local community-based agencies.

The city- and state-funded programs are being evaluated and the five approaches compared.

Examples of Model Programs. The following are typical examples of how these approaches and the six core program components have been implemented in a high school and a middle school.

In a Bronx high school, the SOAR program is housed in its own area as a minischool for 100 eligible ninth graders. They are divided by reading level into four groups; each group attends four academic and two skills-oriented classes (such as TV production, computers, or cartooning). All students are scheduled for tutoring during the first period. Fifty other students, identified during the school year, attend regular classes and are tracked by the program counselor. Two family assistants and one teacher's aide track attendance daily and call absentees or use an automatic telephone dialing machine to contact the families at night. Incentives are used to encourage good attendance. Students receive mugs, calculators, and other prizes in awards assemblies for improved attendance and academic performance and for success in other program-related activities. Periodically, all program students go on a field trip. Through the close tracking of each student's attendance, the small size and family-like atmosphere of the personal school-within-a-school program, academic support, and skills classes, students are encouraged to attend school more frequently and experience more success while there.

A Bronx junior high school has implemented a Strategies type of program for 160 eighth and ninth graders. Students attend regular classes for most of the day but have the added support of special counseling, career education classes, and other activities. As well as taking required subjects, participating students are enrolled in a weekly career guidance class taught by the program facilitator. A drug and alcohol abuse prevention counselor meets with about forty students each week; she also provides special attendance follow-up and school guidance. Students with improved regular school attendance can participate an extended-day program, in which a variety of activities, including field trips and athletic competitions, are offered four afternoons each week and one Saturday each month. Two family assistants and an attendance aide track targeted students' attendance daily and follow up on absentees with calls and home visits. Trophies are presented to students at the end of the year for improved attendance and scholastic achievement, and clock radios are given to students who show improvement in arriving at school on time.

Participants

Because the dropout prevention programs established through the state and city funding initiatives were only in their second year of operation by 1986, information on the students served and the programs' outcomes was limited. In 1985-86, the program's first year, 6,300 high school students were enrolled by midyear. Fifty-five percent were in the state-funded programs, and the rest were in the city-funded programs. Fifty-nine percent were in the ninth grade, 23 percent in the tenth, and the remainder in the eleventh and twelfth grades.

Available information on the state-funded dropout prevention programs shows that the programs were targeting the appropriate group—poorly attending students who also had academic problems. Forty-three percent of the targeted high school students in the schools with the SOAR and Strategies types of programs and 59 percent of those in schools with Operation Success had been absent more than sixty days in the prior school year. Similarly, 63 and 67 percent, respectively, had failed eight or more courses in the previous school year. Fifty-five percent of all targeted high school students were two or more years overage for their grade, and 48 percent were two or more years below grade level in reading. Corresponding data were unavailable for students in the city-funded programs.

Approximately 13,700 middle and junior high school students have been targeted for dropout prevention services in 1986-87; 69 percent are in state-funded programs and the rest in city-funded programs. Forty-seven percent are in the eighth grade, 22 percent in the ninth, and the rest in the seventh grade. Twenty-eight percent of the students are overage for their grade, and 27 percent failed three or more courses the previous year.

Administration

These various dropout prevention efforts are administered separately according to the school level and funding source. The office of student progress oversees the middle school programs, providing technical assistance, reviewing the program components in operation, and monitoring school compliance with the regulations. The office of high school support provides similar oversight for the state-funded high schools. These efforts are coordinated with the office of dropout prevention, which oversees the city-funded high school dropout prevention programs. Through the chancellor's office, the progress of all schools' dropout rates, as well as the performance of the specially funded programs, is reviewed. As a result, only the chancellor's office has an overview of how the programs are integrated and of how all secondary schools are meeting the goal of low dropout rates.

Evaluation

With such a substantial program to start up, it was difficult for the school system to staff and implement all six components in thirty-six high schools and ninety-seven middle schools in 1985-86, the first year the city and state funding initiatives were similarly structured. Of the six core components, the school links and health services were often the last in place. Schools that collaborated with community-based agencies for services also took much longer to get started than schools that did not.

While the programs from the two initiatives are being extensively evaluated and compared, it is too soon to determine any school-specific or school systemwide benefits and improvements. The board of education has established minimum per-

...ance objectives for all dropout prevention programs to determine their effectiveness in improving student attendance and achievement. At least 50 percent of the targeted students must improve their attendance and pass more subjects than the year before; at least 50 percent of the current ninth graders must still be in school three years later; at least 50 percent of the targeted high school students must earn enough credits to advance to the next grade; and at least 50 percent of the targeted middle school students must be promoted to the next grade. It will be interesting to see how well these objectives are met and followed up.

The New York City board of education, through its office of education assessment, annually evaluates the implementation and impact of the state-funded services. A progress report on the state-funded dropout prevention services, made in the middle of the 1985–86 school year, showed positive, although slight, systemwide improvements for the funded schools. Attendance improved, and the number of long-term absentees declined. There was a 13 percent average increase in the attendance of targeted students. More current and extensive evaluation findings on these programs and the city-funded programs, which are being evaluated by an external evaluation team, are not yet available.

The New York City school system has mounted a highly structured, large-scale dropout prevention effort. The attendance improvements and dropout prevention projects are not unusual except in size and scope. One notable aspect of these programs, however, is that they have common features but vary in their approaches and strategies, which are being compared as part of an overall evaluation. One unique strategy being tested is the use of community-based agencies. The program design includes a role for these agencies in coordinating their services and resources with the schools' academic programs.

The New York City dropout prevention effort is not limited to adding programs for its potential dropouts, however. By holding each school accountable for its student dropout rate, the system is encouraging each school to review and restructure its delivery of education to all students. It will be important to see if this accountability system can promote the changes and improvements that reduce schools' dropout rates.

Systemic Approach to Dropout Prevention

Program Components

- Comprehensive dropout prevention program strategy, including attendance follow-up, supportive services, and alternative educational experiences
- Targeting students with the worst attendance
- Establishing school-specific goals for reduced dropout rates
- Long-range plans for dropout service expansion

Program Inputs and Outcomes

- Target population: Middle and high school students with poor attendance in schools with very low attendance rates
- Costs: About $1,000 per student
- Outcomes: Not ascertained

DROPOUT PREVENTION AND RECOVERY PROGRAM
Los Angeles, California

In September 1985, the Los Angeles Unified School District initiated the high-priority Dropout Prevention and Recovery Program to establish school systemwide dropout prevention efforts. According to district plans, the program's overall goal is to reduce the number of dropout and dropout-prone students by increasing the individual school's holding power and by developing alternative educational programs. This goal is implicit in the program's design: it is a long-term, systemwide initiative grounded in local school efforts. The program's strategy is to integrate community services and private-sector involvement with both new and established district programs to improve school retention.

The Los Angeles Unified School District, through local funding, has initiated two systemwide planning efforts to address its dropout problem. First, each school is required to prepare its own dropout prevention plan as part of the required biennial basic activities plan. To aid in this activity, and to assess its dropout problem more systematically, the district has funded the creation of a school-based computerized student accounting system to track attendance and withdrawal in grades 7 through 12. Second, the district is experimenting with several model programs for reducing each school's dropout rate. These pilot projects span all three school levels—eight high schools, eight junior high schools, and eight elementary schools—reflecting the view that the dropout problem must be addressed by a concentrated and coordinated effort throughout the school system. Recently appropriated state monies and changes in categorical grant programs will allow the district to extend its dropout prevention efforts.

As the district evaluates its new dropout prevention and recovery initiatives and reviews systemwide ways of retaining students, it is beginning to take measures to expand educational options for all students. Principals are encouraged to provide alternative programs to meet the varied needs of their students, particularly potential dropouts.

Background

With an enrollment of 578,760 students in 1985-86, Los Angeles has the second-largest public school system in the nation. Like other major urban centers, it is grappling with a student body that is increasingly minority, poor, and educationally disadvantaged. The composition of the student population has altered substantially in the last two decades, from one in which white students predominated (making up 56 percent of the enrollment in 1966) to one in which they are a small minority (19 percent in the 1985-86 school year). In the increasingly pluralistic school system, Hispanics are now the largest ethnic group, representing 53 percent of all students; blacks account for 19 percent; and Asians and Native Americans the remaining 9 percent.

Following a decade of decline, the public school census has risen by 7 percent over the past five years. The most serious problem the district now faces is a shortage of space. Overcrowding exists at every school level, epitomized by the fact that 93 of the 644 schools in the district are year-round schools, including 77 elementary schools.

Over the years, the district has instituted a fairly broad spectrum of programs and options, particularly at the high school level. For example, in addition to regular schools, there are now six "opportunity" schools for students with special problems (for example, pregnant and parenting girls); forty-three "continuation" high schools, each serving about sixty students who have encountered difficulties in regular schools; and eighteen special-focus "magnet" schools, as well as sixty-six "magnet centers" within regular schools. The district is also gradually adding vocational and career options in comprehensive high schools. The continuation schools have developed a contractual curriculum system to encourage students to complete their course work. The district has added automatic telephone dialers in junior and senior high schools to call computer-generated lists of absent students. It has also created student ID numbers to permit long-term student tracking and has developed a computerized student data system. Yet despite these measures, the school system's attrition rate has increased; in 1984 the cumulative rate was 42 percent.

The beginning of the district's Dropout Prevention and Recovery Program can be traced to the summer of 1984, when the board of education and the superintendent of schools declared dropout prevention to be a priority and created a task force to study the problem. In January 1985, the twenty-nine-person task force—composed primarily of the board of education's central office staff, representatives from the teachers' union, and members of education-related commissions—presented its findings, recommendations, and two configurations for a pilot dropout prevention and recovery project. The report recommended a student data system and a standard definition of a dropout, which the board adopted. The school board also adopted the commission's recommendation for a dropout prevention and recovery program; the program was formalized late in the spring of 1985 and financed with slightly more than $1 million from general funds.

This effort was closely followed by state legislation. Senate Bill 65 addresses the state's dropout problem with new policies and funding. The purpose of the legislation is to improve schools' retention of students and reduce absenteeism and truancy by focusing and coordinating existing funding and resources. The legislation also makes new funds available for services to dropouts and potential dropouts. One Los Angeles Unified School District office is coordinating both the local dropout prevention funds and the new state funding, which began in the 1986–87 school year.

Description

The central elements of the locally funded Dropout Prevention and Recovery Program may be summarized as follows:

- The requirement that every school principal develop, with the participation of school staff and parents, a dropout prevention and recovery plan
- The initiation of funded pilot projects in twenty-four schools spanning all three educational levels
- The development and implementation of a systemwide student dropout data collection system for grades 7 through 12
- Coordination with and involvement of community agencies, business, industry, and other central district offices in integrating services and expanding programs.

Every school completes a one-page dropout prevention plan form as part of its biennial basic activities plan. These plans describe the target groups, services to be provided, staffing, and parent education for prevention and recovery efforts. Through a district selection process, some schools receive special local funding to implement their plans. Those that do not are still encouraged to add special services for potential dropouts. The district's policy implementation and evaluation unit and office of compliance may review all schools' plans through their general monitoring and evaluation activities. Preliminary reviews have shown that schools whose plans were not funded, as well as those whose plans were, are trying to set up special programs to keep students in school.

A substantial portion of the special dropout prevention funding goes toward funding these various pilot programs, which were designed according to school-identified needs. In 1985–86, eight high schools and sixteen of their feeder middle and elementary schools were selected to pilot model programs and received $1 million to begin them. The high schools could set up a suggested pilot program (which was to add a dropout prevention adviser, a part-time pupil service and attendance counselor, and a school psychologist) or another option. The elementary and junior high schools could implement an "effective schools" program (a program model piloted by Los Angeles for six years) or whatever program best met their needs. The "effective schools" program's strategies for improving instruction included staff development, emphasis on reading improvement, early assessment of students' needs by subject, regular proficiency testing, instructional pacing, and a structured reading program.

The funding allowed these schools to hire additional teacher aides and to provide in-service staff development and instructional materials. The central district office's only requirements were that the additional funding be focused on dropout prevention and recovery efforts, and that each school target 150 students who were considered at risk of dropping out on the basis of their achievement, behavior, or attendance.

All eight high schools selected by the central administration to receive funding had high attrition rates, according to the 1985 dropout study. The junior high and elementary schools chosen were feeder schools to the selected high schools. Each school, in turn, defined its own student eligibility criteria, which vary considerably among the schools. Approximately 3,600 students are being served, 1,200 at each school level. All twenty-four schools have large numbers of at-risk students, although only a few can be served by the programs.

The local dropout prevention projects differ enormously, ranging from entirely self-contained (school-within-a-school) programs to those that attempt to change school structures, regulations, and staff attitudes. Some projects offer targeted students more intensive academic attention (for example, smaller classes, tutoring, or remediation sessions) or alternative academic programs; others mainstream the targeted students in regular classes on the theory that they must learn to "make it" in the same world as their classmates. All programs provide intensive counseling and tracking. The program coordinator visits each funded school regularly and occasionally holds joint meetings with all twenty-four schools to address implementation prob-' lems or other issues.

The current district's student data system gives each secondary school a computerized attendance report. The system provides easily retrievable, current, and complete attendance records that can be used in attendance and dropout follow-up efforts. The next step is to develop more complete dropout statistics on students in grades 7 through 12, including detailed tracking information on students in the twenty-four pilot schools, by the end of the 1985–86 school year. The ultimate objective is to make a K–12 student database accessible district-wide from terminals in each school by 1990. This will permit more complete tracking of students throughout the school system and quicker follow-up on those who drop out.

The Dropout Prevention and Recovery Program staff, through pilot programs and cooperation with other district offices, identify ways to encourage principals to add alternative education programs to their schools. Among other strategies, they are trying to communicate to the schools that eighteen-year-old students who have not yet completed high school should be encouraged to stay. They are also trying to expand educational options for dropout-prone high school students by allowing students to enroll concurrently in both the Senior High School Division and the Adult and Occupational Education Division. On a limited basis, they are experimenting with putting adult basic education classes in junior high schools and enrolling ninth graders in these classes in the afternoon for remedial instruction. High school students are being encouraged to go to evening school to get caught up in their course work or to have time to work during the day.

Los Angeles will be able to expand the scope of its locally funded dropout prevention program with new state funding and policy changes. In 1986, the California state legislature created a state Pupil Motivation and Maintenance Program (SB-65) and established three ways for the state to address its dropout problem. First, the legislation creates greater flexibility by permitting waivers in school districts' use of categorical aid (such as that for compensatory education and programs for gifted and talented students) and apportionment funds (such as those for continuation education and adult education). Waiving the regulations on the use of these funds encourages districts to develop cohesive programs to serve all high-risk students. Additional funding is made available for the planning and creation of dropout prevention programs.

Second, the legislation allocates funding for services to school dropouts. Part of this money is for alternative work centers established by school districts; the rest is for educational clinics run by local school districts or public or private agencies (none of these are to be established in Los Angeles, however).

Third, the legislation also allocates two sets of funding for use by individual schools. One is for an outreach consultant in each school, who is to develop parent and community support and links with business and industry for school-wide dropout prevention efforts. The other is to be distributed as planning grants to elementary and secondary schools so that they can develop a school plan for staff development, service coordination, early identification and intervention, coordination of existing funded programs, and other activities.

Planning grant funds will come to Los Angeles in cycles and will be allocated for specific combinations of schools. Eight high schools, on the basis of their attrition rates, will be awarded $6,000 planning grants to do a needs assessment and to submit a plan to the state for serving targeted youth. Each high school is to plan and set up a program in cooperation with one of its feeder middle schools and two feeder elementary schools. In the first year, eight high schools with an attrition rate of 38 percent or more and their twenty-four feeder elementary and junior high schools will be selected. Thirty-two more schools will participate each year; currently, five cycles are planned. The combination of state and local planning and funding should eventually reach almost half of the Los Angeles high schools and thus the bulk of the district's dropout-prone population.

Illustrations

Below are descriptions of three typical model funded programs.

Fremont High School. Fremont High School's fall 1985 enrollment of 2,062 was 54 percent black and 46 percent Hispanic. Its 1984 attrition rate of 61 percent was the fourth-highest among the district high schools. With its new funding, Fremont has created the Continued Success Program (CSP). In this program, a coordinator and two college students (employed part-time) provide individual counseling for targeted students. A third college student is employed part-time to follow up on attendance and other administrative matters.

The assumption behind the program's design is that students must function in regular situations, rather than in a special environment. All program students thus remain enrolled in regular school classes. They receive additional counseling and personal attention, including one-on-one counseling with program staff (often in ten-minute conferences between classes) and "adoption" by a school staff member through the program's "Adopt-a-Student" effort. In response to the program's campaign, 76 teachers and others of the 135 full-time staff members agreed to adopt one or more CSP students, providing extra attention on a consistent basis.

In anticipation of the district's dropout prevention funding, Fremont identified 150 dropout-prone students during the spring of 1985, selecting those who were not being promoted and those with attendance, grade, and behavior problems. After consultation with feeder school guidance counselors, some incoming tenth graders were also selected. Parents were notified by mail about their child's selection for the program.

A considerable portion of the coordinator's efforts have

gone into promoting the CSP throughout the community and securing additional resources for the school. Many articles about the school have appeared in local newspapers. The coordinator has appeared on local radio and TV programs. Tickets for special events (such as L.A. Laker games) have been obtained, outside speakers have been engaged for staff development presentations, and negotiations are under way with local businesses and community-based agencies for donations and sponsorship of joint programs.

Hollenbeck Junior High School. Hollenbeck Junior High School's fall 1985 register of nearly 2,300 students (97 percent of whom were Hispanic) is the largest junior high school enrollment in the district. The school is also one of the most overcrowded. For the new pilot programs, the Hollenbeck staff modified a program begun two years earlier for failing ninth graders, called "Save Our Scholars." With the new funding, the staff selected 150 seventh and eighth graders who had been absent more than fifteen days during the fall 1985 semester or who were referred by teachers, counselors, clergy, or others.

The program consists of three components: special core subjects—reading, math, English, science, and social studies—taught in small classes with a student-teacher ratio of 15:1, mandatory tutorial services for any student who falls behind, and two group counseling sessions per week per student, plus individual counseling as needed. By the late spring of 1986, 110 students were participating in the full program. Forty other students were receiving counseling services only. The students were also encouraged to participate in a recreation program funded by Coca-Cola that is open to all Hollenbeck students.

Belvedere Elementary School. According to fall 1985 enrollment figures, 99.9 percent of Belvedere Elementary School's 1,234 students are Hispanic. In the spring of 1985, well before the new funding became available to elementary schools, several staff members began identifying potential dropouts for inclusion in a new "Stay-In-School" program. The school psychologist and several teachers who became program coordinators,

backed by an enthusiastic principal, were the driving forces behind the program. This program was implemented in the fall of
1986.

The staff began with six selection criteria: inconsistent attendance, continual disciplinary referrals to the office, referrals
to the school psychologist, review of student cumulative records, recommendations by teachers, and medical problems
noted by the school nurse. Of 350 students who fit the criteria
and 150 more students identified by teachers, the program staff
had to select 150 students to be served. Lacking knowledge of
any reliable research identifying the characteristics of potential
dropouts at the elementary level, Belvedere staff and the school
psychologist administered a self-concept assessment instrument
to the 500 students. Those with poor self-esteem were selected.
The staff also decided to direct the program to younger students, so they selected 100 students from grades 1 through 3
and 50 from grades 4 through 6.

To avoid stigmatizing targeted children, the staff decided
the program should be an inconspicuous intervention. They selected boredom in school as a possible factor in dropping out
and designed the program to address this with enjoyable activities that focused on self-esteem development. Hence program
students did not know they were in a special program. They remained in their regular classes and were taken out three periods
a week (as other children were routinely for various special activities) for "Magic Circle" classes. Magic Circle is a commer-
cially available "human development" program geared, among
other things, to building self-esteem.

During these sessions, five children from several classrooms in adjacent grades met with a paraprofessional who read
stories aloud and discussed them and supervised arts and crafts
and other activities. The seven paraprofessional group leaders
met weekly with the program coordinators for training and
problem solving. In addition to Magic Circle classes, the staff
regularly contacted the students' parents, developed links with
other community service agencies, and held special events.

Raising students' self-esteem is the one measurable goal
that this program has established. During the fall self-concept

testing, the staff also selected and tested seventy-five other students to serve as a comparison group. The Belvedere staff intend to continue the program for at least three years, replacing students who graduate or transfer, and to test participants each year. This will provide a considerable amount of data on the program's effect on self-concept, grades, attendance, and other performance measurements.

Staffing and Administration

The central district office of dropout prevention and recovery oversees the district's city-funded dropout prevention efforts and will coordinate the new state-funded dropout prevention activities.

Over the years, the district has developed several links with private industry, many of which are now coordinated by its dropout prevention and recovery program office. The Coca-Cola Bottling Company of Los Angeles, an industry-sponsored "Achievement Council," the Los Angeles Area Chamber of Commerce, and the Hispanic Volunteer Council all sponsor or operate programs in the Los Angeles schools that address various student needs and concerns. The program office also works with other school district offices on relevant programs, including the Adopt-a-School Office and the Adult and Occupational Education Division.

Funding

In 1985–86, the Los Angeles Unified School District allocated $1.2 million for a dropout prevention and recovery program. Eighty-five percent was allocated to twenty-four target schools for model programs. School-based pilot project awards averaged approximately $55,000 for high schools, $38,000 for junior high schools, and $34,000 for elementary schools. The district made a commitment to maintain this funding for at least three years. The remaining funds were for central administration staff and an evaluation. Beginning in 1986–87, through the new state-funded dropout prevention program, Los Angeles will receive $160,000 for planning and $1.3 million for outreach consultants for selected schools as part of the first funding cycle.

Evaluation

Late in the spring of 1986, the district began to evaluate the first year of dropout prevention activities. The evaluation is to ascertain whether the newly funded programs targeted dropout-prone youth, to identify the criteria used, and to determine which criteria best predicted whether students would drop out. The evaluation will also describe the characteristics of dropout-prone students. Teachers' opinions on staff development and its impact in the classroom will be collected, and students and parents will be surveyed about the Dropout Prevention and Recovery Program. Interim evaluation results showed that the pilot programs were effective in pupil retention; close to 80 percent of the targeted potential dropouts were remaining in school. In 1987, the evaluation will also identify effective program designs by comparing retention rates of similar groups of students in different schools.

It is too early to assess the impact of either the local, district-funded pilot programs and dropout prevention strategies or the new, state-funded programs. The combination of programs targeting potential dropouts and school system improvement measures should reduce the district's dropout rates. With an emphasis on coordinating existing programs (and with the flexibility made possible by the recent state legislation), the Los Angeles public schools can expand the education opportunities for all students. A unique feature of this school system's approach is its recognition that dropout prevention efforts must span the entire system, elementary as well as secondary grades, and that early identification of students needing assistance will improve the chances of intervening effectively.

Dropout Prevention and Recovery Program

Program Components

- Pilot dropout recovery and prevention programs in elementary, junior, and senior high schools

- Improved systemwide student dropout data collection and attendance tracking
- Systemwide focus on dropout prevention
- Coordination of existing programs and services

Program Inputs and Outcomes

- Target population: 150 high-risk students in each targeted school; all students for other district efforts
- Costs: $280 per student in the city-funded pilot programs
- Outcomes: Preliminary improvement in student retention, attendance, and achievement

8

Citywide Approaches: Looking Beyond the School System for Solutions

With the widespread recognition of the consequences of under-educating a large segment of our population comes a broader sense of responsibility. School systems are now turning to their communities for assistance in addressing the complex needs of potential and actual youth dropouts. While it has become common for selected businesses, community agencies, and even universities to lend resources and support to schools, it is rare for all sectors to join forces in planning to reduce a city's dropout problem. Boston is the first place where citywide support has come together, marshaled by the city's business and educational leaders and structured through an objective-based agreement between the public schools and the leading corporations, universities, and trade unions.

Like the school systemwide efforts, the Boston Compact combines targeted programs for dropout-prone youth with systematic changes in the way the schools' curricula and instruction are organized. But Boston's efforts look beyond the role of schools in improving the retention of students. The Compact acknowledges the importance of expanding employment opportunities and access to higher education, and for that purpose it combines the resources of the business, trade, and university communities.

During the first few years of the Compact, student achievement, attendance, and post–high school employment improved; the school system's dropout rate, however, was not affected. As a result, the participants have redoubled their efforts to determine what organizational and program changes help students stay in school. While they have yet to demonstrate the effectiveness of their solutions, their combined efforts and persistence in trying to resolve this problem are worth imitating.

BOSTON COMPACT
Boston, Massachusetts

The Boston Compact brings together the resources of the Boston public schools and the business, university, and labor communities. It is a formal, objective-based agreement that stipulates the contributions each entity will make to improve education, school attendance, preparation, and post–high school opportunities in employment and higher education for the youth of Boston.

In the four years of the Compact's existence, the school system has combined programs for high-risk youth and career preparation with systemic change in school structure and curricula. The business community's efforts have included pledging priority hiring and developing stronger links between businesses and schools and youth, through school-based employment advisers and summer and part-time jobs.

The Compact evolved from a number of business, school, and university collaborations, many of which came about after Boston's 1974 desegregation order. The unique and well-defined collaboration between Boston's educational and business communities received national attention almost immediately, many groups showing an interest in replicating it. Early evaluations of the Compact's accomplishments indicate that school attendance and business employment of public school graduates have shown improvement and even exceeded the Compact's goals.

The 16 percent annual dropout rate has been obstinately difficult to reduce. The Boston public school system has set forth a systemwide plan while experimenting with a number of pilot dropout prevention efforts, including one sponsored with the Boston Private Industry Council (PIC). The Compact's participants recognize that the hoped-for changes may not be seen for a decade or more.

Background

In 1982, when the Boston Compact was initiated, the Boston public schools were at their lowest point. Boston's economic base, on the other hand, like that of New England generally, had shifted successfully from textiles and manufacturing in the early 1970s to information and technology in the early 1980s. By the mid 1980s, Boston's unemployment rate had dropped to 4 percent, and businesses were competing for applicants to fill entry-level positions.

Several factors throughout the 1970s reduced the ability of the Boston public schools to address their shifting educational needs. Following the 1974 court decision to desegregate Boston's schools, public school enrollment dropped dramatically, while the school population changed from predominantly white to predominantly minority. With declining enrollments came substantial staff layoffs and cutbacks in school resources. More and more students enrolled in Boston's public schools were not graduating. By the early 1980s, about 16 percent of the high school students left annually, and less than 60 percent of any entering high school class was graduating.

At the same time, a number of new school system and business collaborations were tried. The Boston school desegregation case led to several years of bitter conflict over the education of Boston's youth. Anticipating the court decision and recognizing the court's desire for broad community involvement in school improvement, the business sector formed the Trilateral Council for Quality Education as a forum to work with the schools, creating partnerships with all high schools. This council became the coordinating agency for Boston school-business partnerships; in 1985, it became part of the Boston PIC. Following the trilateral council's lead, the court created a formal collaboration between schools and universities as well. These partnerships varied widely in their scope and content and lacked central guidance in deploying resources and assistance most effectively.

Two related business and school projects for improving youth employment substantially strengthened the link between schools and business during the early 1980s: the PIC's Summer Jobs program and the Job Collaborative program. In 1980, through Edna McConnell Clark Foundation funding, the PIC developed the Job Collaborative program, a school-based education and work experience program. Three schools were selected in a competition and started the project in 1981. Laid-off teachers were rehired as PIC career specialists. Their responsibilities were to help place students in private-sector jobs (part-time during the school year and full-time during the summer) after they had successfully completed the two or three job readiness workshops. Initially, each specialist worked with fifty students per school. By 1986, there were career specialists in fourteen of the seventeen high schools, each working with up to 150 students.

The PIC's Summer Jobs program has been placing youth in private-sector summer jobs since 1981. The PIC solicits summer job placements for the students trained by the career specialists through preemployment activities. Companies are asked to pledge jobs or to contribute the salary equivalent for a student to be placed in a private-sector job. In 1986, the PIC placed 2,600 students in summer jobs around the city, demonstrating that opportunities exist in the business community.

These collaborative efforts and informal relationships created a climate in which the Compact could develop. Many of the key actors who helped to create the Boston Compact were in city government, major corporations, and the school system administration and had worked together over the years, often on youth employment issues. Several had worked on federal education and on employment and training in the Carter administration. The strong leadership and direction of the new superintendent of schools helped to win the confidence and thus the participation of the Boston business community, a powerful constituency for the public schools. The superintendent, wishing to improve the partnership between business and the schools,

had consultants draft a plan in cooperation with the PIC and selected members of the Boston business community. This plan
became the Boston Compact.

In September 1982, Boston's public schools and the business community formally launched the Boston Compact. This
was a joint pledge to improve the quality of educational preparation and the access to employment for Boston's public high
school students. According to the terms of the Compact, the
Boston public schools agreed to reduce the dropout rate by 5
percent annually and to work toward annual increases in attendance and performance on standardized tests. The schools
would improve basic-skills training and performance on required
minimum competency reading and math tests for all 1986 graduates. The business community's side of the bargain was a
promise to give priority in hiring to a specific number of public
school graduates, to increase the number of summer jobs for in-
school youth, to sign up at least 200 companies for a priority
hiring effort, and to expand the PIC's Job Collaborative program.

The premise of the agreement was that efforts for middle
school and high school students should be tied to clearly per-
ceivable employment experiences and opportunities. Implied
was the belief that the poor academic performance of Boston
public school students is a community and business responsibility.

The first signers of the Boston Compact were a group of
twenty-five chief executive officers from the city's largest companies who were concerned about the problems of Boston's
public schools. Since the late 1950s, these leaders had worked
cooperatively as a coordinating council, known informally as
the Vault, on areas of social responsibility. Their prominence in
the business community drew others to join the compact. The
only strong complaint was from the black community, which
requested and received assurances that minority youth would
be employed in percentages reflective of their proportion in
the school system. With this addition, the Boston Compact was
officially signed on September 22, 1982.

The agreement later was expanded to include colleges and

trade unions. In November 1983, the Compact added an agreement with the Presidents' Steering Committee, which represents twenty-five colleges and postsecondary schools. These higher education institutions agreed to the goal of a 25 percent increase by 1989 in the college enrollment of Boston public school graduates. To help with this goal, the business community later formed the Action Center for Education Services and Scholarships with corporate and foundation grants to put advisers in high schools to assist seniors with postsecondary plans and financial aid applications and to provide a "last dollar" scholarship fund. This fund is to fill the gap in financial aid for college.

In December 1984, twenty-seven unions, through the Boston Area Trade Union Council, pledged openings in apprenticeship programs for Boston school graduates on the condition that the schools offer union-designed curricula for training. Each union was to work out individual letters of agreement with the schools, committing the unions to school visits and presentations, provision of transportation to application sites, and waiver of the application fees.

Description and Participants

The Boston Compact, while in fact only an agreement, has fostered a series of efforts to improve school attendance and basic-skills performance, decrease the number of school dropouts, increase the number of school graduates hired by Boston businesses and companies, and increase graduates' opportunities for higher education and trade apprenticeships. The PIC board of directors, which includes the chairperson of the Vault, the chairperson of the chamber of commerce, and the superintendent of schools, serves as a forum for regular discussion of Compact-related activities and accomplishments.

In the first few years of the Boston Compact, a planning group made up of business and school system representatives met regularly. The Boston Compact Steering Committee, a thirty-member committee representing various Boston interests and co-chaired by the superintendent and a business representative, oversees the Compact's progress. This committee also serves as a public forum and reports on how well the Compact's objectives are being met and on newly developed programs. A dropout prevention task force is a work group of this committee.

Since the beginning of the Boston Compact, the public school principals have focused their efforts on improving students' reading performance and school attendance. Less attention has been given to how each school can reduce the number that drops out. In part, this focus follows the school system's new criteria for graduating seniors. Beginning in 1985–86, students must have an 85 percent or better attendance rate and a score of at least 64 on the Degrees of Reading Power test (a standardized reading achievement test) to graduate.

The Boston public schools have made significant progress since the Compact was launched, although they have yet to achieve their original goals. Between 1982 and 1985, average daily attendance increased from 78.3 percent to 84.8 percent, an improvement of almost 10 percent in three years. While the high schools were still performing below the national average on basic-skills tests, students in grades 9 and 10 showed steady improvement. Ninth graders increased their performance from the 42nd to the 48th percentile on reading tests and from the 32nd to the 50th percentile on math tests. The dropout rate, however, did not decrease.

The Boston business community has had greater success in meeting and even exceeding its goals. By 1984, 336 businesses had signed the Boston Compact's priority hiring pledge; 607 of the 1984 graduates had been placed in Boston Compact firms. Summer job placements increased from 522 in 1981 to 1,766 in 1984, an increase of more than 300 percent. The Job Collaborative program, which provided in-school youth with part-time work, grew from 90 students in three schools to 550 students in twelve schools. By 1986, fourteen of the seventeen Boston high schools had full-time PIC career specialists who helped to follow up more than 1,000 students who had been in the PIC work-study jobs and the Job Collaborative program.

The initial success of the Boston Compact has encouraged its sponsors to redouble their efforts to reduce the school system's dropout rate. The Compact's designers have focused specific attention on the dropout problem, recognizing that it is not easily solved by attendance and employment incentives. The various planners acknowledge that short-term school system changes that improve student attendance and academic achievement do not simultaneously improve schools' holding power; stiffer requirements and attendance policies may actually discourage students from continuing school and thus increase the likelihood that they will drop out.

Two kinds of efforts are under way to address the problem systemwide while serving those students at risk of dropping out. The first is a major effort by the Boston public schools to initiate a dropout prevention plan that will bring in broader community resources and address structural barriers to retention. The second is a pilot dropout prevention program sponsored by the business community through the PIC in cooperation with the Boston public schools. This program, Compact Ventures, targets high-risk ninth graders in two high schools.

The Dropout Prevention Task Force. In response to its persistently high dropout rate, the Boston public schools, with the assistance of the Boston business community, sponsored a citywide conference in the spring of 1986 to present a plan for reducing the dropout rate and to develop broad-based involvement. The newly hired superintendent not only embraced the objectives of the Boston Compact begun under his predecessor but pushed for more substantive change throughout the school system to address the dropout problem on all instructional levels.

The working outline for the conference proposed two measurable goals: to reduce the number of dropouts by one-half and to double the number of dropouts enrolled in alternative education programs or schools. The assumption underlying the proposed effort was that dropping out of school reflected a number of problems that were a community responsibility. Systemwide improvements were needed in the schools to improve the chances that students would succeed, particularly for students in grades 6 through 12. These efforts included evaluating programs to determine their effectiveness and exploring fundamental changes in the way education was delivered.

The working plan identified a number of aspects of school organization that may inhibit learning. It proposed basic education programs for students in grades 6 through 9 along with individual educational plans. The plan identified several alternative programs that could be expanded and evaluated. It also reviewed a range of human services that could be expanded and coordinated with services for dropouts.

As part of this approach, the Dropout Prevention Task Force was created. The task force has called for structural changes in each school, early identification of potential dropouts, division of high school courses into semesters (so that students failing in November do not fail for the year), and broader coordination of school and work. The school system also hopes to direct local funding toward dropout prevention projects. However, many proposed changes are organizational or structural and do not require funds. The long-term objective is to have both a central dropout prevention plan and individual school plans.

Compact Ventures. Compact Ventures was developed in 1984 by the PIC in response to a Massachusetts Office of Economic Affairs grants competition. The PIC was awarded $392,000 to set up a program to reduce the dropout rate of high-risk ninth graders substantially and to improve their academic achievement through supportive services, reorganization of the ninth grade into clusters, and employment opportunity incentives. Once the program obtained funding, the PIC solicited proposals from city high schools and selected two schools in a competition. The PIC staff then worked closely with the school staff to adapt the program model for each school. At English High School, ninth graders were organized into three clusters of one hundred students each, housed together in one area of the high school. Extra teaching staff were assigned to maintain a low student-teacher ratio. At Dorchester High School, all targeted students were assigned to one cluster and rotated together through a core set of classes.

In both schools, the program focuses on basic-skills improvement and provides substantial in-school support. Student attendance is tracked daily, and a system of rewards and incentives reinforces good attendance. Both schools offer summer job placements as incentives for good attendance and achievement and provide tutoring assistance for those who are doing poorly academically. In the cluster program, the teachers are better able to work cooperatively to address individual problems, to team-teach, and to prepare an instructional plan that meets the students' needs.

Incoming freshmen are selected for the program if they have failed three or more courses, have been absent frequently, or have erratic grades and attendance; 75 percent must be income-eligible. Each school selects 120 students for the program. Half are selected during the summer and visited by the youth worker, who explains the program to them and their parents. The rest are referred to the program during the school year by guidance and teaching staff.

In one high school, about half the students come in daily for tutoring, for which they receive course credit. Once a week, the tutoring classes are used for skills development and life-skills exercises, such as planning a budget and looking for a job. Students can come after school three days a week for more tutoring, although few do. All students are assigned to one of two youth workers who track their attendance and provide group or individual counseling and referrals. After each marking period, the youth workers review the students' report cards and discuss with them how they are doing and how to improve their grades. In some cases, they make education contracts with the students as a motivational device. The youth workers also promote self-esteem building through group counseling, trips, and other group activities. Parents are encouraged to attend regular meetings.

Compact Ventures is funded by the Massachusetts Office of Economic Affairs, through discretionary Job Training Partnership Act funds of $392,000 per year. The staff at each school includes a project director, two counselors, a tutoring coordinator, part-time tutors, and volunteer college students and business employees. In both schools, the staff work closely with the teachers and counselors assigned to the ninth graders. The Compact Ventures program has become a resource for the staff as well as the students, supporting the teachers in working with problem students and providing discretionary resources for school activities and field trips. The program students like having a place in the school where they can go. The tutoring and counseling services support the teachers in their instructional role.

At the end of the first year, the two project high schools found they had substantially reduced their ninth-grade dropout rates, from 22 to 11 percent at Dorchester High School and from 25 to 16 percent at English High School. Both schools had also improved their reading test scores, by 6 percent at Dorchester and 14 percent at English.

The Boston PIC did a process evaluation of its Compact Ventures program on the basis of which it is making several adjustments. The PIC has decided to follow a case-management approach more closely, to make services to youth more standard, to use the counselors more like career specialists, and to have more routine contact with the students. The PIC plans to contract with local community organizations to provide the program support services.

Staffing and Administration

Although it is a joint effort by a wide range of education officials and businesses and universities, the Boston Compact is primarily monitored by the Boston PIC and the Boston public schools. The PIC works as a clearinghouse through which firms are recruited to hire Boston public high school graduates preferentially and to offer part-time or temporary employment to in-school youth. With the expansion of the PIC's Job Collaborative program, career specialists were added in each school to improve students' career preparation. The PIC currently has thirty staff members working in the Boston public schools through the Job Collaborative program and Compact Ventures. Together they oversee the jobs component of the Boston Compact.

The Boston school system undertakes the school improvement activities, coordinated through an office under the superintendent. When the compact was being designed, the school system appointed school partnership coordinators, called development officers, in each high school. They became each school's liaison for all local compact activities as well as for activities with each school's business partner.

Since the compact's beginning, a strong effort has been made to have the schools and their staff feel responsible for the program. At the end of each school year, school principals meet with their faculty to develop new plans for the coming year. They work through planning teams that represent a cross-section of school constituencies to address specific compact goals. The plans are reviewed by the compact's steering committee and a group of educators and civic leaders and are then awarded small discretionary grants.

Funding

The Boston Compact is not a single entity but is enacted through several programs, each of which is separately funded. It has been estimated that about $600,000 is spent each year on related activities. Much of the compact's work has been funded by in-kind contributions and the pro bono efforts of the Boston businesses, universities, and labor unions.

Evaluation

Of its four primary goals, the Boston Compact has been most successful in improving the employment of its public high school graduates. Some progress has been made in improving school attendance and academic achievement, but the high school dropout rate persists unchanged.

An improvement of almost 10 percent in school attendance was accomplished between 1982 and 1985, below the hoped-for 15 percent. During the same period, performance on reading tests rose to the 48th percentile and on math tests to the 50th percentile, close to the national averages. But the annual school dropout rate, to be reduced by 5 percent each year, has remained at 16 percent. The school system's focused effort with the greater Boston community to explore ways of reducing its dropout rate should prove to be successful. In the meantime, target programs like Compact Ventures ought to help in retaining those most likely to drop out.

Periodically, the PIC summarizes business participation in and contributions to the Boston Compact, demonstrating both short- and long-range gains. In November 1985, the PIC reported that 823 of the 1984 graduates were placed in permanent jobs as part of the Boston Compact, 10 percent more than the goal of 750 and almost double the number placed in 1983, the compact's first full year. This number includes only those students hired through the Boston Compact hiring campaign; other graduates found jobs on their own or through other agencies. By March 1985, nine months after graduation, 90 percent of the placed graduates were working full-time or were enrolled in an education program. Seventy-six percent of these graduates belonged to minority groups, reflecting the program's effort to place minority students as promised in the compact. Over two-thirds of the working students had already received raises.

In 1985, the PIC, in cooperation with the Boston public schools, contacted 2,300 of the 2,978 1985 graduates in a survey of their postgraduation status. Fifty percent were in school, 59 percent were working, 7 percent were unemployed, and 5 percent were in another activity, such as the military (some respondents were in more than one category).

Other cities have replicated the compact in consultation with the Boston staff or on their own. Oakland Alliance received a $20,000 Clark Foundation planning grant to develop a similar program in Oakland, California, by adding a career specialist and a corporate volunteer program to its organization.

Boston Compact

Program Components

- Collaborative effort between the school system and other city-based interests to reduce the schools' dropout rate
- Measurable objectives for school improvement and youth

employment opportunity, agreed to by the Boston public schools and Boston businesses, universities, and labor unions
- Dropout Prevention Task Force, for school systemwide and communitywide planning
- Pilot dropout prevention program for high-risk ninth graders

Program Inputs and Outcomes

- Target population: Boston public high school students
- Costs: Not calculated
- Outcomes: Increased attendance, achievement, and hiring of graduates

9

What Works Now and
What Is Needed
for the Future

The size and complexity of our nation's dropout problem demand many solutions—to serve those who have quit school, to prevent those who are dropout-prone from leaving, and to reduce the need for dropout services by improving the organization and delivery of public education. The fourteen programs described here offer useful, workable options for achieving these objectives. Available evidence suggests that these programs can be replicated in full or tailored to fit local program needs.

The programs cover a range of approaches to the dropout problem, from short-term supplemental programs to comprehensive district- and citywide strategies to make schools more responsive to students' needs. Collectively, the fourteen programs illustrate important lessons in what works and how. They demonstrate ways of tailoring services to special needs through access, curriculum content and structure, staffing and resources, and funding. Above all, they show that many program options are needed to tackle the job of helping potential and actual youth dropouts to finish high school and preventing more students from becoming dropouts.

Designs and Objectives

All the programs implicitly or explicitly reflect common short- and long-term goals. The short-term goals are to keep youth engaged academically, to give them basic reading and computational skills, to expose them to the world of work, to prepare them for employment, and in particular to see that they graduate from high school or get a GED. The long-term goal is to see the youth become employed, particularly in a growth industry, or go on to advanced education or training.

Program objectives that are specific and well understood are important in any effective school program but essential in working with dropout-prone or out-of-school youth. It is likely that these youth feel alienated from schools, as researchers have suggested. Program objectives that are directed toward their achievement and postprogram success will strengthen students' participation as well as provide a focus for clarifying and integrating all program components.

The programs differ in their emphasis on preventing students from losing interest in school and on encouraging those who have left to try again. Those programs designed as preventive measures keep potential dropouts or other at-risk students in school by redressing early the personal, academic, and social circumstances that may cause alienation or an inability to continue school. These programs enhance students' chances of graduating from high school by giving them support and assistance in the areas they need most.

Other programs focus on students who have officially or unofficially dropped out of school. Encouraging young people to return to school or to enroll in an alternative program requires incentives—such as guaranteed jobs, vocational training, or a focused academic program—to motivate students toward high school completion as well as to provide academic and social support. Finding these youth may depend upon good connections between and referrals from other educational and social agencies.

All programs give considerable attention to student retention. They recognize that what may motivate a young person to return to school or to try an alternative program may not be sufficient to keep him or her in school. Incentives for short-term accomplishments such as attendance and academic improvement and a transitional step into employment can help to sustain students throughout a program.

Target Population

The programs target four groups of dropout-prone and out-of-school youth. The first consists of children and youth who have family and personal backgrounds and educational experiences similar to those of youth dropouts (such as course and grade failures and disciplinary problems), but who are still interested in school. In the hope of preventing them from becoming disenchanted with school, programs have been designed to help the students with their educational problems and encourage them to continue to view high school graduation as an attainable goal. These programs range from the pilot projects in Los Angeles that identify high-risk elementary school students to the screening program for preadolescent boys in the Texas health clinic program and the mentoring program for high school juniors and seniors in Atlanta.

The second group is similar to the first, except that these students appear to have given up on school already; through frequent lateness and absenteeism, they seem to be drifting away from school. The programs try to reinterest these students in staying in school and assist them with the academic deficits they have typically incurred by their truancy and lack of interest. Several programs, from the supportive efforts of the Twelve-Together program to the comprehensive approach of Project COFFEE and Rich's Academy, focus on students like these.

The third group consists of those who are unable to continue with school because of external circumstances, such as teen motherhood or the need to work. For them, lack of motivation or interest in school is not the problem as much as personal circumstances that they cannot juggle along with school. The school-based day-care center in Detroit and the evening school program for migrant workers in Washington State illustrate approaches in which the school systems have modified their regular programs to accommodate these needs.

The fourth group is made up of those who have given up on school and dropped out. These youth may be frustrated enough with their limited employment options to want to complete high school, but a regular high school program is no longer feasible. The privately managed educational clinics in Washington and the community-based alternative schools and youth centers in Chicago illustrate two ways of offering these young people a chance to complete their high school education by an alternate route.

Although each program is designed for one of these four target groups, its focus is likely to be further restricted, usually for funding and service reasons. Programs may define their target population by demographic factors, such as age (being in a particular age-group or being overage for a grade), family income (being low-income or AFDC-eligible), or family structure (being from a single-parent household or in foster care). They may select participants on the basis of academic factors, such as class rank, number of courses or grades failed, or achievement test scores. Finally, they may consider social and personal characteristics, such as poor school attendance, discipline problems, or the lack of personal motivation and self-esteem. These factors have been found to be highly correlated with dropping out of school and they provide a means of selecting an appropriate student population. Most programs consider two or more of these characteristics to select those most in need of program support, although several have balanced this by screening for students who are at least somewhat motivated.

Service Strategies

The fourteen programs contain, in different amounts, four service components: basic-skills remediation, world-of-work exposure, supportive services, and personal development. These are the services that potential and actual youth dropouts need most to sustain them in a program and prepare them to complete high school (or get a GED) and enter the work force. The differences among the fourteen programs are reflected in the scope and structure for delivering these component services, the curriculum and instruction, and operations and management.

Because of their disrupted or disenfranchised relationship with school, potential and actual youth dropouts are commonly deficient in basic reading, writing, and computational skills. Such deficits limit their ability to take advantage of other—particularly employment-related—program services. The fourteen programs offer a variety of approaches to basic-skills remediation, ranging from classroom instruction and tutoring to competency-based, computer-assisted instruction. Even the supplemental service programs that depend upon the participants' regular high school programs for the academic component—Twelve-Together and Adopt-a-Student—encourage the youth participants academically.

All the programs address the participants' employment preparation. This is done either through limited job preparation and world-of-work exposure or, more directly, through work experience in internships, part-time jobs, or occupational training. At the very least, each program helps youth to understand the kinds of jobs available (particularly in growth fields) and their own employability. Generally, the programs offer basic information on how to apply for and keep a job. The focus on job preparation and some vocational training serves two objectives. First, since these youth are among the least able to enter the work force if they drop out of school, job preparation improves their postprogram options for employment. Second, it helps the youth recognize their own limited employability, thereby motivating them to stay in the program.

Employment preparation and basic-skills improvement are necessary and complementary. Previously evaluated youth employment and training programs have demonstrated that the guarantee of a summer job and part-time work encourages youth to return to school but is insufficient to keep them there. The results suggest that this incentive must be tied to basic-skills remediation. The programs presented here make this link with successful results. Comprehensive programs, such as Job Readiness and Project COFFEE, are able to offer work experiences of graduated difficulty and responsibility; advancement depends on successful performance in both the academic and employment-related activities.

Another core component is to improve self-esteem and increase responsible behavior. This is done in two ways. One is through the counseling services and the mentoring and peer-group relationships created by the program. The other develops self-esteem indirectly through the efforts of the staff. The small program size and the close relationships between staff and students that generally result can promote a positive self-image and an "I can" attitude that often is not achievable in larger programs or schools. In these close relationships, it is easier to emphasize good attendance and other qualities of responsible behavior critical to success in school and employment.

Finally, all programs reflect an understanding that dropouts face many personal and social problems and therefore require additional resources to help them remain in school or complete a program. The problems related to a low-income background can interfere with a young person's ability to achieve academically. The more that dropout prevention and service programs can help youth cope with these and other personal problems, the more likely they are to succeed. This assistance can be provided through program-sponsored counseling and guidance or through direct referral to service agencies for housing, welfare, or medical needs. The school-based health clinic is a rare example of a program that is capable of offering medical and social services on the site instead of by referral elsewhere.

These four core program components are delivered by one of three methods. One is to have all students participate in the same set of classes and services. The second is to offer a menu of services from which students and staff can select to shape a program for each student. Both approaches set up alternative programs or services for a target group. The third approach is more general and indirect. It entails changing the school delivery system to respond to the varied educational needs of students, with the intention of reducing the need for a separate dropout prevention program.

Collaboration and Funding

The program approaches have been selected to illustrate collaborative efforts among interested parties to serve youth dropouts or to redirect potential dropouts. Most often, the collaborations are between the schools and other organizations or businesses; not all programs are managed by schools. Through such cooperation and the use of different resources, the programs have effectively tapped funds and in-kind contributions to create and sustain themselves.

Three programs were created by business groups in cooperation with the public school system: Adopt-a-Student, Job Readiness, and the Boston Compact. Community agencies started three programs: the Adolescent Primary Health Clinic, Twelve-Together, and the Summer Youth Employment Program. Only two programs are examples of local school-initiated programs: the Murray-Wright High School Day-Care Center and Project COFFEE. The remaining four programs are a mix of state, private, and local school district initiatives.

From the start or by solicitation later, the programs have created well-defined roles for the private sector and for community-based agencies. These collaborations entail the sharing of resources, building on the particular strengths that each participating agency can contribute. In one program, for example, the business sector recruits adult volunteers to provide support and world-of-work exposure. The community-based agencies, on the other hand, have strong links to a range of supportive services, a means of recruiting volunteers, and the flexibility to match their resources to a school's program.

Several programs illustrate creative funding and support efforts. While it is important for programs to become institutionalized for long-term support, as seven programs are (either partially or fully), it is also critical that all appropriate and available funding sources be tapped. A major problem for any community or school is finding the resources to design and deliver a program. These programs show how to generate opportunities from unlikely sources (for example, using a department store for a classroom and work site) and how to tap federal, state, and local funds not typically used for education. The school-based day-care center and the health clinic's program for teen mothers are both examples of such a creative use of public funds; both are partially supported by state-administered federal social services grants.

At least four programs either receive federal job training money for summer youth employment placements or are guaranteed slots in other similarly funded programs. Four programs have benefited from generous in-kind contributions from business, ranging from token gifts used as prizes for academic and attendance improvement to space for program activities and computer hardware and software. Two programs, Twelve-Together and Adopt-a-Student, depend substantially on volunteer business people to serve as mentors or group leaders. Finally, at least one program, Rich's Academy, uses workers on loan from city social service agencies as its counseling staff.

Intervention programs typically are more costly to operate than regular school services. By definition, the supplemental service programs are far cheaper to run than the more comprehensive ones, particularly because they are staffed in part by volunteers. But the comprehensive in-school programs are not exorbitantly more expensive than regular school programs. For example, Project COFFEE has a per-student cost of $3,000, which is only 20 percent higher than the estimate of $2,400 per student in regular day programs. The other two comprehensive in-school programs, Job Readiness and Rich's Academy, have even lower per-pupil costs. All three programs, however, are very dependent on contributed resources for work experience or counseling.

The comprehensive out-of-school programs are also not as costly as might be expected. The cost per student in the Educational Clinics averages $636. The Alternative Schools Network, while unable to estimate its per-student costs, probably has similar academic expenses, plus the expenses for employment preparation.

The more expensive program models are those that address barriers to continued education. Day-care centers and health-care clinics require facilities and staffing that can be costly to provide. In contrast, the systemwide approaches entail program and operating charges that may not require additional funding but do entail staff and administrative time and effort.

Effectiveness and Evaluation

The existing evidence for effectiveness is quite favorable. When measures are available, they all show good retention of students, improved attendance rates, academic gains, and good completion and graduation rates. Most of the programs have addressed the major flaws of earlier program models by putting a strong emphasis on basic-skills improvement and on helping students cope with personal and family problems, while emphasizing employment preparation.

Program directors, staff, and students gave their own explanations of what made their programs successful and why. Almost uniformly, program directors attribute the success of their programs to the dedication and commitment of their staff. Students point to the caring and supportive environment of the program and the chance to work at their own pace. And while it was not always enunciated, these programs have a clear purpose for all staff and participants. These observations speak of qualities important to any program's effectiveness.

Unfortunately, program evaluation is too often a low priority, almost never included as part of a program. Since the programs are not intended as experiments, they fail to document whether a selected strategy yields appropriate results. Only one program evaluation used a comparison group. None randomly assigned students to the program or a comparison group (which is very difficult politically for schools to do). In several cases, preprogram and postprogram evaluation information was collected only from a nonrandom portion of the participants, making it difficult to generalize the findings to the entire population. Only four postprogram follow-up surveys were done and three of these were conducted three to six months after the program, when only a short-term impact was measurable. One program did a five-year follow-up evaluation but had an inadequate comparison group. Few of those programs that performed evaluations measured the services each participant received and related them to the outcomes.

A lack of adequate evidence does not mean that a program is ineffective. But the limited data and lack of evaluation designs for the reviewed programs make it difficult to determine whether good results illustrate program effectiveness and whether poor results are a matter of insufficient evidence, poor program implementation, appropriate but inadequate services, or inappropriate services. The analysis of each program and the comparison of their strategies also raise questions about which features are most important. Only systematic evaluation can ascertain the usefulness of each feature.

Concluding Observations

The fourteen programs reviewed here offer the core features that education and employment and training experts are now recommending for success in serving youth dropouts. Two additional features, however, can reinforce and extend the effectiveness of each program: creating a role for parents and following up on participants after they leave the program.

Some programs involve students' parents to a limited degree, but most merely invite parents to meetings or contact them about students' lateness and absenteeism. In some programs, such as Twelve-Together and Adopt-a-Student, staff or volunteer advisers make home visits to become familiar with their students' own environment. One program, Job Readiness, has tried to create a more formal role for parents by sponsoring parent-education workshops. These strategies represent only limited contact with students' families, however.

Research on school dropouts points to the influence of each parent's educational attainment and the effect of the home and community environment on how much young people learn and retain. These findings suggest that students' families can be important partners in dropout prevention and service programs.

Although it is very difficult to involve parents in school activities, particularly when their children are adolescents, more attention should be given to bringing them in.

Another way to extend the successful impact of these programs is to provide follow-up counseling and assistance after the youth complete them. The severity of the personal and economic problems characteristic of dropout-prone and out-of-school youth points to a need for postprogram support. In particular, such assistance would be helpful as the young people make the transition into their first jobs or continued education and training. The supportive and encouraging environments created by these programs should not end abruptly.

Reducing our nation's dropout rate will not be easily accomplished. Specific policy and program steps, many of which are already under way, should have a significant impact, however. In particular, recognition of the diverse causes and consequences of dropping out has lead to greater collaboration among schools, businesses, universities, and social agencies to address the dropout problem. Such collaborations have begun to bring more resources to bear and have generated creative solutions for dropouts' education and employment needs.

Program planning should concentrate on two points: how best to address the individual needs of targeted students and how to reduce the dropout rate in the larger community. The fourteen programs illustrate useful approaches to designing programs for targeted students. Collectively, they present a framework for recognizing the different segments of a community's dropout-prone population and for providing services tailored to the circumstances of each segment. What is proposed here, then, is not that schools and communities look for a single solution or consider only a segment of the dropout problem but that they integrate several services and programs.

It is tempting to look for an ideal approach. If one existed, it would be the comprehensive strategy of school systems such as those of New York City and Los Angeles and of cities such as Boston. Their attempts to reduce the dropout rate are not limited to stopgap measures for a few of the many potential dropouts in their areas. Rather, they combine short-term

programs for dropout-prone youth with a review of ways to restructure their general school delivery system to expand the
educational opportunities for all students and thereby reduce
the need for more dropout prevention services.

Implications for the Educational System

Our nation's support of universal education through high
school means that young people are entitled to the opportunity
to reach a certain level of academic achievement. But as this
examination of dropouts illustrates, not all youth are equally
capable of taking advantage of this opportunity. While public
schools cannot guarantee that all students will attain a basic
level of academic skill, they do have the responsibility to make
this attainment achievable for as many students as possible.

School districts and communities are already adding a
variety of programs to assist potential dropouts. They are also
beginning to change institutional factors that may discourage
students from staying in school. To be sure these two kinds of
efforts are successful and fill existing service gaps, however,
more systematic planning and coordination of services is needed.

Most of all, schools are in the best position to intervene
early. One approach is to target youngsters who might later be
at risk of dropping out; Los Angeles, for example, is adding
educational and supportive services for targeted elementary
school children. The other approach is to redirect existing
school strategies by placing low-achieving, disadvantaged young
people in summer school programs, linking educational programs to future employability through school-to-work transition programs, and incorporating vocational education into
dropout prevention efforts.

Implications for the Employment and Training Field

Youth dropouts are a target for federally funded employment and training services. They have proved costly and difficult to serve, however, primarily because of their educational
deficits (Orr, 1987). But this target group is too large a portion

of our youth population and too necessary for business and industry to be ignored.

Some of the fourteen programs show how other funding sources—such as adult basic education, literacy assistance, and social services monies—can be used for basic skill remediation when federal funds are limited, thereby reserving job training funds for employment preparation and job-specific training. The programs demonstrate that this is a feasible and effective approach.

Collaboration

The intense public interest in the causes and incidence of dropping out has led to greater acceptance of the idea that there is a broad social responsibility for the dropout problem. What remains unclear is what service system ought to be the focal point for remediating the educational and employment problems of dropouts and dropout-prone youth. Public schools are emerging as the system with primary responsibility for young people who are at risk of dropping out. Actual dropouts are served primarily by public employment and training programs, because federal funding for these services is the only major funding source available for this population.

A more formal role must be created for other service systems and interested groups to share in the responsibility of serving actual and potential dropouts. The public education and employment and training systems lack adequate resources to provide all services to those who need them. Other agencies can provide complementary services. For example, public and private social service agencies have expertise in handling personal, family, and social problems and have connections to other referral agencies. They are also more accustomed to drawing on volunteers for assistance. Many businesses, while not service providers, are often interested in helping with local community problems through personal or in-kind contributions.

Current education, employment and training, and community agency programs for dropout prevention and service are often fragmented. Rarely do these agencies plan collaboratively or systematically about a service population. Such collaboration would clarify the extent to which the dropout problem exists and help to engender broader public and private program support.

Integration and coordination of services around youth dropouts is not a simple accomplishment, however. The richness of services that results when the efforts of several agencies are combined is politically expensive, as was aptly pointed out in a comment on a policy report on the dropout problem (Hahn and Danzberger, 1987). The turf problems that result from the separate goals, procedures, and identities of collaborating agencies and institutions can be more costly program barriers than a lack of resources and commitment. This is equally true for collaborations between businesses and service agencies.

This caution is meant to serve as a guide, not a deterrent, for those undertaking collaborative efforts. The current lack of educational and employment and training resources for serving youth dropouts and dropout-prone youth makes it necessary to collaborate and coordinate services to construct sufficient program support. In addition, the complex problems facing these young people require the expertise of more than just education and employment and training programs.

Financing Dropout Prevention and Service

Existing funding resources fall short of meeting the needs of the dropout and dropout-prone population. These dollars can be stretched when various services and funds are combined to create a comprehensive program. The fourteen programs discussed above offer critical lessons in ways to combine funding resources and tap in-kind contributions.

Inadequate funding is probably the greatest barrier to schools and communities that want to add new programs. The projections of potential lifetime earnings lost and social costs incurred when young people drop out argue for the benefit of helping these youth complete at least their high school education. But the savings will not accrue to the schools and other agencies that provide the programs. School districts and their communities have therefore been slow to acknowledge the true size of the potential and actual youth dropout population. The fourteen programs show, however, that services directed toward this population, when integrated into existing school programs and supplemented with contributed resources and assistance, are not exorbitantly expensive. Fortunately, not all the program solutions depend on rearranging existing services. State and local governments are beginning to allocate new funds to this population.

Evaluation

The importance of systematically testing the effectiveness of various strategies and programs cannot be overemphasized. This is especially true in the field of dropout prevention and service, where many efforts seem to be taking place all at once. Only by evaluating the outcomes and comparative benefits of dropout prevention and service programs can we learn which strategies and services are most appropriate and beneficial for the different segments of the dropout population.

A number of important design questions emerge from the survey of fourteen programs. For example, to what extent is any strategy effective in bringing adolescents back into school? How much are these adolescents motivated to return by their limited employment opportunities and how much by the program options? What features or strategies are effective in keeping them in school or a program once they are reenrolled—the minischool or small-group atmosphere, the incentives and rewards, or the work experience? Furthermore, while it is obvious that these youth need supportive services, it is unclear how much any strategy to address their affective and social needs helps to keep them in school. For example, could a supportive strategy be sufficient if used alone, or is it effective only in combination with other services, such as work experience and basic-skills remediation? Finally, if more of a particular service were available to each student, what additional benefits might it yield?

Systematic evaluation should not be limited to learning

how a program works and what its outcomes are. There has been too little assessment of the relation between available services and the dropout-prone young people that need them. The one operational weakness we noted in all fourteen programs was ignorance of the overall need for services in a community, the program's success in reducing this need, and the total number of young people who could benefit from this or a similar program. The comprehensive schoolwide and school systemwide approaches of Los Angeles, New York, and Boston have begun to do this. But we have yet to develop a program that benefits more than a segment of the dropout-prone youth while addressing the needs of out-of-school youth as well.

Appendix A:
Research Background

After careful research and reviews of programs, the staff of the Structured Employment/Economic Development Corporation (SEEDCO) have selected fourteen policy and program strategies that help to keep potential dropouts in school or help those who have left to complete their education. We particularly looked for programs that exhibited inventive combinations of resources and funding and that varied in their target populations, basic service components, initiating institutions, and funding.

To identify potential program models for investigation, we reviewed SEEDCO's files of state and local JTPA service strategies for dropouts. We also did a lengthy library search that included reviews of the Educational Resource Information Center (ERIC) system, the National Diffusion Network, and published books and articles on dropout prevention, dropout service efforts, general alternative programs, and employment and training programs. Unfortunately, these sources yielded little beyond anecdotal descriptions of programs and hypothetical strategies for successful programs.

The most useful resources were educators, academics, and employment and training specialists. We interviewed over fifty individuals who recommended state and local initiatives to pre-

vent students from dropping out of school. Their recommendations included national demonstration efforts, newly initiated
state and local programs, and continuing programs as well as referrals to other researchers reviewing program strategies.

From a list of fifty to seventy-five state and local programs, we selected examples from both rural and urban areas in
different parts of the country. We deliberately chose programs
in communities with severe dropout problems, thus weighting
our selection toward cities. In our review of strategies we devised a framework of programs and prevention efforts, which we
used to select examples. We found that target populations,
types of service strategies, initiating and sponsoring agencies,
and methods of funding all differed dramatically. Many of the
programs we selected display a combination of strategies but
are used in this book to illustrate only one.

Each of the fourteen programs was contacted and visited
by a team of two field interviewers. They spent one or two days
at each site, interviewing key program staff and administrators
and a few students and observing classes and other activities.
Wherever possible, they also interviewed outside funders and
evaluators. All used a structured interview guide, which is included in Appendix B, to collect comparable information on all
projects. Questions focused on each program's nature and composition, history and development, funding sources, state and
local agencies involved, target populations, program strategies,
evaluation results, relations with other local education and employment and training programs, leadership, and general community support. We explored how multiple services are coordinated and delivered and, in cases where multiple funding is
used, how each funding mechanism operates, the limitations of
each, and the advantages of combining several funding sources.
Facts necessary to other policy and program officials wishing to
replicate or adapt these strategies were also collected.

The teams prepared an in-depth summary case study of
each program that was sent to the program directors, and occasionally to other program specialists, for review and comment.
The final verified case studies were then revised, reviewed again
by the program directors, and then edited for this book.

The identification of programs, preparation of the taxonomy, and drafting of the case studies were carried out with input from a six-member advisory group. The members represent national organizations, agencies, and universities concerned about the dropout problem.

Appendix B:
Field Visit Guide

SEEDCO Dropout Program Study: Field Visit Guide

Date_____

Program _____

School/Agency_____

Address _____

_____

Persons Interviewed

Name   *Title*   *Address*   *Telephone*

History/Background of the Program
(How did the organization or community address dropout
retention or recovery in establishing this program?)

1. Give the history of the program's development.

    a. What was the origin of the program for this community? What was the origin of the program model (internally or externally designed)?

    b. How was the need for this program determined (for example, review of dropout rates, availability of grant funds)?

    c. Give a chronology of the events and the key elements (for example, date of origin, staff, leadership, funding, students, and community support).

    d. Which outside consultants, advisors, funders, business and community agencies, and other organizations were involved in the establishment of the program and under what circumstances?

    e. What were the major incentives and constraints or obstacles and how were they managed?

    f. What changes in the design, goals and objectives, expectations, and outcomes have occurred over time?

2. About the mechanical aspects of establishing the program— were there any licensing requirements, need for school board approval, or special space or equipment needs? If so, please describe.

3. Describe the dropout problem within the school district/ community.

4. What other kinds of programs in the school/district/community serve dropouts or provide dropout prevention services (for example, focusing on absenteeism, remediation, school suspension, or teen pregnancy)? How is the project related to these other programs?

Program Characteristics
(How do the program's design and operation address the needs
of dropouts or at-risk youth?)

1. What are the program's goals and objectives?

2. Describe each program component and how students participate in it, for each of the following. If possible, obtain copies of the curriculum. Describe how each relates to the overall program goals and objectives. How are these designed to address the specific needs of the population served? How do students become eligible for each program component? How are students' needs diagnosed?

    a. academic units

    b. nonacademic units

    c. world-of-work orientation, work experience

    d. counseling, social services

    e. attendance improvement

    f. medical and health care

    g. food and nutrition

    h. transportation

3. How are the various program components coordinated for each student and for the program as a whole?

4. What is the organizational setup for the program?

    a. What is the context?

    b. What is the physical layout of the program? How many sites are there?

    c. What are the hours of program operation? How long does the program run?

    d. What special materials are needed for this program?

    e. How is each student's progress evaluated?

5. If school-based, how does this program fit within the regular school? Can students in the program participate in other school activities and vice versa? What other services are available for participants and how are students eligible for these?

6. Describe a typical student's day.

7. What problems do students have with the various program components and how does the program respond to the problems?

8. What related problems do students have that interfere with their school/work performance? How, if at all, does the program address these problems (for example, drug or alcohol abuse, housing, family-related, or other problems)?

9. What postprogram services exist for the student participants (for example, job placement, follow-up)?

10. How is the students' progress evaluated?

11. What are the plans for expanding the program or adding services?

12. What special materials or books does your program require for its operation? Discuss.

Population Served/At-Risk Population Targeted

1. How do students get into the program?

    a. Who is the program intended to serve?

    b. Who is eligible for this program?

    c. How are students recruited or informed about the program's existence?

    d. How are students selected to participate? How are their needs diagnosed?

e. Is there a waiting list and if so how is it managed? What services are offered to students who make requests but are not enrolled in this program?

2. How many students are served by the program? What are the demographic characteristics of the program and the school/community? How many students are enrolled and what is their background in terms of SES, race/ethnicity, sex, or special needs (such as, limited English proficiency or physical handicap)?

		Program Participants	*School*
Total		_____	_____
Grade	a.	_____	_____
	b.	_____	_____
	c.	_____	_____
	d.	_____	_____
Male		_____	_____
Female		_____	_____

Other program participant characteristics:

3. What are the program policies for students' positive and negative terminations from the program?

a. When does a student successfully complete the program?

b. Under what circumstances are students asked to leave, without completing the program?

c. How are those who drop out of this program followed up?

Staffing and Management

1. What is the staffing and administration of this program and how does this arrangement address the service needs of dropouts or at-risk youth?

a. Describe the number and responsibilities of staff

members. What special qualities must staff persons exhibit to be hired for the program?

b.   Describe the student:staff ratio.

c.   How is the program administered/managed?

d.   How does the program fit into the school district's, PIC's or other agency's organizational structure?

2.   Describe the external staff resources and support services.

a.   What are the roles of the school principal, central headquarters staff, school board, and others in the continued operation of this program?

b.   How is the business community involved in the program?

c.   How are the community social agencies involved in the program?

d.   What is the role of the students' parents in this program? Are special services or components provided for them? Explain.

e.   Does the program use volunteers and if so, what kinds and under what capacity? How are they recruited?

f.   Describe the other interagency relationships in support or operation of the program.

3.   Describe any special staff training needed for serving students in this program.

4.   Describe the organization that is directing this program.

Funding

1.   How is the program funded? Describe the types of funding and give proportional amounts—federal, state, local, private and in-kind; describe the specific requirements for services or students for each funding source.

2. How is outside funding obtained?

3. What future funding sources will the project be using and for what purpose?

4. What is the program's annual budget?

    a. personnel: _____

    b. facilities: _____

    c. equipment, materials, supplies: _____

    d. maintenance: _____

    e. insurance: _____

    f. transportation: _____

    g. consultants: _____

    h. other (specify): _____

5. What in-kind resources or materials are used for this program?

6. How are the funds administered?

Evaluation/Program Assessment
(How effective is the program in addressing the dropout problem?)

1. What evidence exists that this program is effective in keeping students in school, recapturing dropouts, and helping students complete high school?

    a. Obtain evaluation criteria used and learn how they are measured for each program objective and for the program's overall goal. If a formal evaluation has been done, obtain a copy. Discuss how the evaluation was done and by whom.

    b. Discuss how the evaluation results address the effectiveness of the program and its components in meet-

ing the program's goal of serving at-risk youth/drop-
outs.

    c.   Discuss how the findings have been followed up.

2.   Which program components contribute most to the program's success in retaining dropouts and helping them to
complete their education? Can these be replicated elsewhere?

3.   What evidence exists to suggest that the intervention would
work with other kinds of students, in other settings, and
with other staff? That is, is this project unique to this environment or can it be replicated successfully elsewhere?

4.   Where has this program been replicated? Briefly describe
the circumstances.

Overall Program Impressions

1.   How does the program "feel"?

    a.   Does it seem structured, stimulating, and so on?

    b.   Do students and staff seem to enjoy it?

    c.   Is the staff diverse in background?

    d.   Is the space neat, clean, in good repair? Is it excit-
ing and interesting? Does it have sufficient resources?

2.   Is there something special about the program that could be
replicated? Something special that could not be replicated?

Adolescent Interview

1.   Describe a typical day in your program.

2.   What courses are you taking?

3.   What other activities do you participate in?

4. What are your plans after you finish the program? Give specific examples.

5. How did you find out about this program?

6. What were you doing at that time?

7. Why did you drop out of school (or want to)?

8. What other programs do you participate in?

9. What do you like about this program?

10. How do you think it can be improved? What else would you like to see offered?

11. If this program did not exist, what would you do instead?

# Appendix C: Contacts for Dropout Prevention Programs and Services

Adolescent Primary Health Care Clinic
Ms. Donna J. Bryant, Executive Director
Urban Affairs Corporation
2815 Reid
Houston, Texas 77026
(713) 222-8788

Adopt-a-Student
Dr. Claude George, Director
Office of Job Development
Atlanta Public Schools
Atlanta, Georgia 30312
(404) 522-3174

Alternative Schools Network
Mr. Jack Wuest, Executive Director
Alternative Schools Network
1105 West Lawrence Avenue
Chicago, Illinois 60640
(312) 728-4030

Boston Compact
Mr. Ted Dooley, Executive Director
Boston Compact
Boston Public Schools
26 Court Street
Boston, Massachusetts 02108
(617) 726-6200

Ms. Jacqueline Rasso, Business Partnership Manager
Boston Private Industry Council
110 Tremont Street
Boston, Massachusetts 02108
(617) 423-3755

Dropout Prevention and Recovery Program
Mr. Pete Martinez, District Coordinator
Dropout Prevention and Recovery Program
Los Angeles Unified School District
450 N. Grand Avenue, Room H-221
Los Angeles, California 90012
(213) 625-5608

Educational Clinics
Ms. Barbara Mertens, Director
Private Education
Office of the Superintendent of Public Instruction
Old Capitol Building, FG-11
Olympia, Washington 98504
(206) 753-2562

Job Readiness Program
Ms. Pat Morgan, Associate Director
Chicago United
116 South Michigan Avenue
Chicago, Illinois 60603
(312) 236-3769

Murray-Wright High School Day-Care Center
Mrs. Jean Booth and Mrs. Jenethel Cummings
Department of Home Economics
Murray-Wright High School
2001 West Warren Avenue
Detroit, Michigan 48208
(313) 494-2553

Office of the General Superintendent
Detroit Public Schools
5057 Woodward Avenue
Detroit, Michigan 48202
(313) 494-1078

Project COFFEE
Mr. Michael Fields, Director
Project COFFEE
Oxford High School Annex
Oxford, Massachusetts 01540
(617) 987-2591

Rich's Academy
Dr. Claude George
Office of Job Placement
Atlanta Public Schools
Atlanta, Georgia 30312
(404) 552-3174

Mr. David Lewis, President
Exodus, Inc.
1011 West Peachtree, N.W.
Atlanta, Georgia 30309
(404) 873-3979

Secondary Credit Exchange Program
Mr. Jim Rigney
Facilitator/Trainer
Migrant Education Program
Superintendent of Public Instruction
Old Capital Building, FG-11
Olympia, Washington 98504
(206) 753-1031

Summer Youth Employment Program
Ms. Sylvia Beville, Vice President for Policy
Office for Job Partnerships
181 Hillman Street
New Bedford, Massachusetts 02741
(617) 999-3161

Systemic Approach to Dropout Prevention
Ms. Jody Spiro, Executive Assistant to the Chancellor
New York City Board of Education
110 Livingston Street
Brooklyn, New York 11201
(718) 935-2796

Twelve-Together
Ms. Donna Lovette
Metropolitan Detroit Youth Foundation
16810 James Couzens
Detroit, Michigan 48235
(313) 864-0700

References

Appalachian Regional Commission. "ARC Workshop Showcases Practical Programs for Dropout Prevention." *Appalachia,* 1985, *18-19* (6-1), 1-21.

Atlanta Cities in Schools Program. Statistical report for the 1983-84 school year. Atlanta, Ga.: Exodus, Inc., n.d.

Baker, P., and others. *Pathways to the Future. Vol. 4: A Report on the National Longitudinal Surveys of Youth Labor Market Experience in 1982.* Columbus: Center for Human Resource Research, Ohio State University, 1984.

Barro, S. M. "The Incidence of Dropping Out: A Descriptive Analysis." Unpublished paper, SMB Economic Research, Inc., Washington, D.C., 1984.

Berlin, G. "Towards a System of Youth Development: Replacing Work, Service and Learning Deficits with Opportunities." Statement at the Congressional Hearing on Youth Employment and the Job Corps, Subcommittee on Education and Labor, Washington, D.C., Mar. 26, 1984.

Berlin, G., and Duhl, J. "Education, Equity and Economic Excellence: The Critical Role of Second Chance Basic Skills and Job Training Programs." Unpublished paper, Ford Foundation, New York, 1984.

Berlin, G., and Sum, A. "American Standards of Living, Family Welfare, and the Basic-Skills Crisis." Unpublished paper, Ford Foundation, New York, Dec. 1986.

Betsey, C. L., Hollister, R. G., Jr., and Papageorgiou, M. R. (eds.). *Youth Employment and Training Programs: The YEPDA Years.* Washington, D.C.: National Academy Press, 1985.

Borus, M. E. "Why Do We Keep Inventing Square Wheels? What We Know and Don't Know About Remedial Employment and Training Programs for High School Dropouts." Unpublished paper, Rutgers University, 1984.

Bullis, B. "Dropout Prevention." Unpublished paper, Stanford University, 1986.

Catterall, J. S. *On the Social Costs of Dropping Out of School.* Palo Alto, Calif.: Stanford Policy Institute, Stanford University, 1985.

Catterall, J. S., and Stern, D. "The Effects of Alternative School Programs on High School Completion and Labor Market Outcomes." *Educational Evaluation and Policy Analysis,* 1986, *8* (1), 77–86.

Committee for Economic Development. *Investing in Our Children.* Washington, D.C.: Committee for Economic Development, 1985.

Cusick, P. "The Effects of School Reform on the Egalitarianism of the Schools." Paper prepared for the American Educational Research Association Project. East Lansing: Research Contributions for Educational Improvement, Michigan State University, 1984.

Education Commission of the States. *Reconnecting Youth.* Denver: Education Commission of the States, 1985.

Goodwin, D., and Muraskin, L. *Regulating Excellence: Examining Strategies for Improving Student and Teacher Performance.* Alexandria, Va.: National Association of State Boards of Education, 1985.

Hahn, A., and Danzberger, J. *Dropouts in America.* Washington, D.C.: Institute for Educational Leadership, 1987.

Hahn, A., and Lerman, R. *What Works in Youth Employment Policy?* Washington, D.C.: Committee on New American Realities, National Planning Association, 1985.

Hammond, R., and Howard, J. P. "Doing What's Expected of Youth: The Roots and the Rise of the Dropout Culture." *Metropolitan Education,* 1986, *2,* 53-71.

Institute for Educational Leadership. *School Dropouts: Everybody's Problem.* Washington, D.C.: Institute for Educational Leadership, 1986.

Kolstad, A. J., and Owings, J. A. "High School Dropouts Who Change Their Minds About School." Unpublished paper, Office of Educational Research and Improvement, U.S. Department of Education, Washington, D.C., 1986.

Legislative Budget Committee. *Report on Educational Clinics, Program Years 1982-1984.* Report no. 85-7. A report to the Washington State Legislature. Olympia, Wash., 1985.

Levin, H. M. *The Educationally Disadvantaged: A National Crisis.* Working Paper no. 6. Philadelphia: Public/Private Ventures, 1985.

Lyke, B. "A Short Summary of the Previous Federal Dropout Prevention Program." Unpublished paper, Congressional Research Service, Library of Congress, Washington, D.C., 1985.

McCarthy, W. *Reducing Urban Unemployment: What Works at the Local Level.* Washington, D.C.: National League of Cities, 1985.

McDill, E., Natriello, G., and Pallas, A. M. "A Population at Risk: The Impact of Raising Standards on Potential Dropouts." Unpublished paper, Johns Hopkins University, 1985.

Mann, D. "Can We Help Dropouts? Thinking About the Undoable." *Teachers College Record,* 1986, *87* (3), 3-19.

Manpower Demonstration Research Corporation. *Findings on Youth Employment: Lessons from MDRC Research.* New York: Manpower Demonstration Research Corporation, n.d.

MDC, Inc. *The States' Excellence in Education Commissions: Who's Looking Out for At-Risk Youth.* Chapel Hill, N.C.: MDC, Inc., 1985.

National Center for Research in Vocational Education. "Research Findings on Dropouts." Paper prepared for the National Conference of State Legislatures, San Francisco, Mar. 7-8, 1986.

National Coalition of Advocates for Students. *Barriers to Excel-*

lence: Our Children at Risk. Boston: National Coalition of Advocates for Students, 1985.

National Commission on Excellence in Education. *A Nation at Risk: The Imperative for Educational Reform.* Report to the Nation and the Secretary of Education, U.S. Department of Education. Washington, D.C.: National Commission on Excellence in Education, 1983.

National Governors' Association. *The Five-Year Dilemma.* Washington, D.C.: National Governors' Association, 1985.

Office of Educational Research and Improvement. *Digest of Education Statistics 1985–86.* Washington, D.C.: U.S. Department of Education, 1986.

Orr, M. T., with Clark, C. J. "A Study of the Procedural Coordination and Program Linkages Between the Job Training Partnership Act and Education with a Special Emphasis on Youth Dropouts." Unpublished report, Structured Employment/ Economic Development Corporation, New York, 1987.

Owings, J. A., and Kolstad, A. J. "High School Dropouts Two Years After Scheduled Graduation." Unpublished paper, Longitudinal Studies Branch, National Center for Education Statistics, U.S. Department of Education, Washington, D.C., 1985.

Peng, S. *High School Dropouts: Descriptive Information from High School and Beyond.* Washington, D.C.: National Center for Education Statistics, U.S. Department of Education, 1983.

Peng, S. "High School Dropouts: A National Concern." Paper prepared for the Business Advisory Commission of the Education Commission of the States, National Center for Education Statistics, U.S. Department of Education, Washington, D.C., 1985.

Rumberger, R. W. *High School Dropouts: A Problem for Research, Policy, and Practice.* Palo Alto, Calif.: Stanford Education Policy Institute, Stanford University, 1986.

Treadway, P. G. "Beyond Statistics: Doing Something About Dropping Out of School." Unpublished paper, Stanford University, 1985.

U.S. Bureau of the Census. *Statistical Abstract of the United States: 1985.* (105th ed.) Washington, D.C.: U.S. Government Printing Office, 1984.

U.S. General Accounting Office. *School Dropouts: The Extent and Nature of the Problem.* Washington, D.C.: U.S. General Accounting Office, 1986.

Washington State Legislature. "Chapter 180-95: WAC Educational Clinics." WAC 180-95-010. Feb. 8, 1978.

Weber, J. M. *The Role of Vocational Education in Decreasing the Dropout Rate.* Report submitted to the Office of Vocational and Adult Education, U.S. Department of Education. Columbus: National Center for Research in Vocational Education, Ohio State University, 1986.

Wehlage, G. G. "At-Risk Students and the Need for School Reform." Unpublished paper, National Center on Effective Secondary Schools, University of Wisconsin, Madison, 1986.

Index